THE FACE OF THE NUDE

JOHN BROPHY

the face of the nude

a study in beauty

TUDOR PUBLISHING COMPANY
New York

Published in the United States by Tudor Publishing
Company, New York, 1968

Library of Congress Catalog Card Number: 68-57797

Printed in Holland

CONTENTS

LIST OF COLOUR PLATES

PREFACE

This book is a consideration of the nude and of the ways in which Western artists, at various times and places, have depicted the face in relation to the human body. The plates are arranged in approximate chronological order — approximate because it is not always possible to say in exactly what year an old picture was made. They are arranged in pairs: in one plate the whole of a work (or a sizeable portion of it if it is exceptionally large) is reproduced: on the opposite page a head, usually the head of the principal nude figure in the whole composition, is reproduced so that the reproduction is, within a few millimetres, the same size as the head in the original.

A high degree of fidelity has been aimed at and, whenever possible, the colour plates have been compared with the originals and all feasible adjustments made. It is not possible, however, to make a reproduction in colour of a large painting and catch *all* the colours precisely. This is for the same reason that, if one looks in a museum or gallery at a large picture from some distance, so that it seems small, its appearance is slightly changed; the colours seem to be both darkened and simplified. There is a natural law governing this matter, and no one can overthrow it. In these pairs of plates, because of this natural law, it is the one showing the face that conveys more precisely what the artist actually painted. On the other hand, all these reproductions are exempt from most of the hazards that beset the original. Not only paintings but sculptures, however skilfully they are displayed, vary in tone and colouring with the time of the day, the season of the year, and the state of the weather, and they may become obscured by accumulating layers of dirt while they wait their turn for cleaning and restoration. None of this applies to a book such as this in which the colour plates can always be examined, in whatever kind of lighting the reader prefers, and are always seen at their best. For permission to reproduce the various works of art the thanks of publisher, author, and printer are due to the private owners and to the directors and governing bodies of the art institutions.

THE FACE OF THE NUDE

chapter 1

Other creatures grow their own clothes as fur or feathers, as scales, or a thick protective skin. Man alone can make himself a wardrobe, and man alone, therefore, when he leaves off clothing, looks and feels naked. There may be an element of shame in the human attitude towards nakedness quite separate from any emotion aroused by religion or morality. It is not so easy, as some have believed, to establish (except as an opinion) that the pagan peoples of the ancient world had no sense of shame about nakedness. Very few people, however, are likely to feel distress or anxiety merely because they are without clothes. Nakedness is quite correct in conditions of privacy. It is the presence or the threatened arrival of other people, especially of strangers, that bothers us.

This suggests that our attitude towards nakedness may be more primitive than we think and have its origin in fear. From a biological viewpoint the most important distinction between man and other animals may be his ability to make tools and clothes and weapons; and for one of our remote ancestors to be surprised in a state of nakedness — that is to say, without tools or clothes or weapons, defenceless as a hermit crab out of its shell — must have been an intensely alarming experience. Translate such alarm into terms of modern civilization and it becomes acute social embarrassment — and embarrassment is exactly what nakedness in certain circumstances sets up in real life.

In art it is different. An artist may be a drunken, foul-mouthed wastrel — although many, perhaps the majority of artists have in fact been respectable citizens — but works of art, once any novelty they may possess has been blunted by time, carry enormous prestige. Even those people who dislike art, or are not interested in it, dare not say so publicly. Works of art, once accepted by contemporary taste, are generally regarded as beautiful and deserving of serious study. Not only that: works of art are exempted from conforming to those regulations governing public decency that every community enforces. The 20th century, in Western Europe and North America at least, has been a libertarian age in which, decade after decade, laws and customs governing dress and public behaviour have been relaxed, modified, or completely abolished. Men and women dress for games and to take the sun in summer wearing vestigial garments which even 50 years ago would have caused a riot. Nevertheless, there is still a convention: the wispy coverings permissible on the seashore or in a private garden become improper if they are worn in the streets. Unless the body is removed indoors or more adequately clothed, the police in almost any city or large town will intervene.

Certainly, any man or woman who appeared in the streets stark naked would be arrested as fast as the police could be brought to the spot. Yet in the same streets we can all look as much as we please at nude sculptures, at a male or female figure standing high on a plinth so that it can be seen the better, or at a group of figures ornamenting a fountain and close enough for passers-by to touch. There is a clear discrepancy in our attitude to art and real life. It may be objected that the reason the police do not enforce decency on public statues is that neither limestone nor bronze very much resembles live flesh. The objection, however, is not a valid one. That is shown by the fact that the greatest art galleries are public galleries, where anyone and everyone can walk about and look at naked men and women pictured in full colour and in considerable detail. To visit art galleries is not only permitted but encouraged as a praiseworthy activity.

The fact is that we take for granted the exemption of art from certain restrictions as if it were a law of nature. It looks as though we, the community, believe — or at least we assume — that art has the power to transform the unacceptable into the praiseworthy. To stand naked is one of the most private things a person can do. The presence of strangers would make it at best embarrassing, at worst indecent. It is the power of art which alone can enable us to be at ease in the apparent presence of other people's nakedness. Art does a great deal more than this, of course, but this is sufficient to mark the distinction between art and pictorial pornography whether in books or on the stage or the cinema screen. Although unsophisticated people paying a first visit to, for example, the Louvre or the Kunsthistorisches Museum in Vienna, sometimes show in their faces that they are startled by what they see displayed in paint, they are quick to realize that the other visitors, and the attendants, take it all for granted. Art establishes a special convention for itself. It demands to be experienced as objectively as possible, and by aesthetic standards, and in doing so it seems to emancipate us from many of the inhibitions normally operating in our minds.

Exactly what proportion of the great paintings and sculptures of the world show one or more nude figures cannot be precisely calculated. For one thing, differing interpretations may be placed on the word 'nude': some people may think that unless the whole body is shown in the picture, and is completely uncovered, it is not a nude; for other people this would be a pedantic, or hypocritic, distinction, and the fact that parts of the body are screened by other figures, by objects such as trees, by small pieces of drapery, or by conveniently placed draperies, only emphasizes the general effect of nudity. At certain times and places, in the Byzantine Empire and in Western Europe during the Middle

Ages, the human body was, as a general rule, depicted closely clothed or not at all. Except when the nude was thus forbidden, because it was regarded as sinful, painters and sculptors have agreed that, as a subject, the naked human body offers the greatest challenge to an artist's skill. From the Renaissance to the present century the study of the human body, its structure and organization, has been as central to the pictorial arts as to medical science. The Life class, with male or female model stripped and posing on a central platform, was the most important aspect of the work of the academies, the forerunners of art schools, and even painters like Hogarth and Constable, who rarely if ever painted a nude figure, continued to attend such classes long after they had made their names as independent artists.

Two reasons, not conflicting but complementary, can be cited for the pre-eminence of the nude at least from the 15th century onwards. The first reason has to do with the fact that the greater part of the skin covering the human body is either hairless or has such fine short hairs that they make practically no difference to the appearance of the skin. An animal, a flower, a bird, a fish, a snake may seem — these are matters of taste and opinion — as beautiful as a naked human being and just as difficult to draw or to paint. In fact, however, the human body, perhaps because it is so elaborately organized inside, presents a unique problem in art. Its movements may or may not be as supple and sure as those of some animals, but the play of muscles is more visible in undulations of the skin surface, and its repertoire of movements is infinitely greater. Few things in nature — some fruits perhaps, and motionless water — reflect light as subtly as the bare human body, but fruits have no independent power of motion while water takes form only from what contains it. The nude therefore has for centuries been recognized as the stiffest of all tests of artistic skill, and many a painter and sculptor — Michelangelo and Leonardo da Vinci are the outstanding examples — has devoted almost the whole of his adult life to drawing as a means to understanding such things as how the breast moves when the arm is raised above the head or how toes and instep and ankle interplay in the apparently simple operation of taking a step forward.

The second reason for the pre-eminence of the nude over a period of 500 years — the years during which Western Europe moved from a mediaeval organization and a mediaeval outlook into scientific developments that now have hurled us into the Space Age — is that artists remembered that under every costume there was a naked human being and that the costume would look quite different if it were merely hung on a peg or draped over a clay figure. For most religious pictures,

for portraits, for most landscapes with figures, and for pictures of contemporary life, the artist's task, or a great part of it, was to show people wearing clothes. Often the clothes were highly ornamental, adorned with jewels, ribbons, laces and other ornaments; at some periods they were secretly padded out, over the arms or the shoulders, at other periods over the thighs, and at others over the buttocks, so that it would be impossible to deduce even vaguely the shape of the body beneath. Nevertheless, the precept was instilled, and believed, and put into practice, that to make a satisfactory painting or drawing of a clothed human being it was necessary first to make a preliminary drawing of a nude. It was not always the person who was to be depicted fully dressed who posed for the nude sketches, and we may suspect that some of the great ladies of the past were discreetly flattered by portrait painters who, not content with 'improving' their faces a little, while retaining a likeness, used nude drawings of professional models as a foundation for the legs and torso in the finished picture.

Court painters in countries where art was not granted the customary exemption from strict conventions of dress, like 16th-century Spain or Mid-Victorian England, either tried to dispense with the nude, to their own detriment as painters, or took themselves off to Paris or Florence or to some favourable environment where they could hire models by the hour or attend life classes without fuss. A certain amount of mystery hangs around Velasquez in this regard. There is only one genuine female nude among all his output of paintings, the 'Rokeby Venus' at the National Gallery, London. The Rokeby Venus was perforce excluded from the colour plates illustrating this book because the face of Venus is seen only in the mirror that Cupid holds, and there the image is all too realistically blurred, as if it had been breathed on or exposed to steam. This is so brilliantly done that it is hard to believe Velasquez painted no other nudes. Drawings by him are excessively rare, and again it is hard to believe that he did not practise drawing intensively, both for study and for experiment, if not in Spain, then during his visits to Italy. There is no evidence in support, but the suspicion seems almost to suggest itself that some unknown person must at some time, probably soon after the painter's death in 1660, have destroyed a number of Velasquez drawings, and perhaps some oil sketches also, in the belief that, because they were nudes, they were *ipso facto* improper.

It is easy enough to make a comparison between puritanic, death-engrossed Spain and the tolerant ways of Italy and France, and remind ourselves that drawing from the nude was practised, and brilliantly practised, by Pisanèllo (fig. 1) at Verona before the Renaissance had properly got under way. We can recall that some

Antonio Pisanello (c. 1395–1455/56), Studies of Nudes and Annunciation Group, 22 x 16.5 cm. Rotterdam, Museum Boymans-Van Beuningen.

1

of Raphael's most revered Madonna pictures are each the culmination of a series of experimental and progressive drawings, beginning with studies of the nude, and that French art earned an international reputation for its erotic quality when the Palace of Fontainebleau was being built and decorated and has maintained that reputation ever since. This, however, is to select some historical facts and ignore others. Puritanism is not confined to certain places and times, and it would be wiser to regard it as a permanent part of human nature. That aspect of puritanism that involves fear and disapproval of sexuality, and therefore of depictions of the nude, manifests itself, especially when it appears as a reaction against license, in many, if not all, countries. In Italy, the Florentine Botticelli, before he died, came under the puritanic influence of Savonarola and more or less stopped painting, while Michelangelo was helpless to stop a puritanical Pope from commanding Daniele da Volterra — one of Michelangelo's former

pupils — to paint loin cloths and other draperies on those figures on the Sistine Chapel ceiling that were nude. In France, where the fashion for the Fontaine-bleau style had exhausted itself, the nude was made academic and formal, and a later reaction, against rococo frivolity, can be seen in the painting and sculptures of the Revolutionary and Empire periods. This is not the same thing as puritanic suppression, but it sometimes achieves similar ends. Napoleon seems to have had an odd taste for allowing, or encouraging, the neo-Classic sculptor, Canova, to depict him in the nude. He stands, in white marble, larger than life size, at the foot of a staircase at Apsley House (Wellington Museum) in London. A bronze casting is at the Brera Gallery, Milan. Napoleon's sister, Pauline Bonaparte, was also portrayed by Canova, naked to the waist; the marble is at the Borghese Gallery in Rome (Plate 69). A painted portrait of Pauline, by Robert Lefèvre, dated 1806, can be seen in London; ironically it also is at

15

the museum that commemorated Napoleon's conqueror, Wellington. It shows her wearing a dress so transparent that the nipples are clearly visible. As if in competition, Napoleon's second wife, the Empress Marie-Louise, was by tradition the original of the full-length nude Venus in Prud'hon's large painting, 'Venus and Adonis', in the Wallace Collection, London. French puritanism is not, however, the contradiction in terms it may seem and has often made its influence felt in the pictorial arts as in literature; it was not Manet's habit of maintaining mistresses that shocked Paris, nor even the open secret that they were sometimes his models, but something too crude and direct, perhaps, in the pose and the facial expression of the nude girl in the picture which he called 'Olympia'.

chapter 2

A nude, however well drawn or painted, is not necessarily stimulating to sexual desire. Communal ideas of what is beautiful vary from time to time and from place to place, and personal opinions differ just as much and often more surprisingly. There is also the fundamental distinction between the typical, or presumably average, attitude of a man towards any female nude and the typical attitude of a woman towards the same nude. A man's attitude may be summarized, if he considers the nude in question to be beautiful, as a mixture of aesthetic and sexual interest in proportions which will vary with the man, the picture, and the occasion but will never be susceptible to scientific measurement. It is probable that a woman's interest in the same picture will be a blend of the same two elements, equally variable and indefinable, but with the important difference that the sexual interest (unless it is itself to some degree sapphic) is quite differently aligned: it will be interest in the painted nude not as a hypothetical object of desire but as an example, successful to the point that at least a painter took the trouble to depict her, of that kind of female nudity that men find attractive. Exactly what women think and feel about nude pictures of other women is not easy to discover. Women either cannot or will not disclose adequate information, and, at a guess, one might conclude that for various reasons most of them prefer to leave the matter obscure in their own minds.

On the surface the attitude of men towards the nude is, by comparison, lucid and could be expressed as a proposition in logic: a young and healthy female wearing no clothes is desirable; therefore, a picture of her must be desirable. Aesthetic appreciation of this sort is crude and superficial, and, although there is a long tradition that urges men to demonstrate their masculinity by a

hearty jolliness whenever a sexual subject comes up for discussion, manners are changing. While there is less hypocrisy about the sexual element in responses to the nude, other aspects, both subtle and objective, of those responses are being recognized. At a period when the vulgarities of 'strip tease' entertainments have spread like a skin disease almost everywhere, it is paradoxically true that the aesthetics of the female nude in art has never been so widely understood. Pictures of naked men present a different problem. Except for those with a tendency towards homosexuality, observation indicates that most men take practically no interest in the masculine nude. This may be because they live their lives in an instinctive, unself-critical way, and for them the very idea of human beauty is bound up with the idea of sexual desire. When desire is not aroused there is no perception of beauty and, indeed, not much curiosity. The distinction is very noticeable at auction sales of pictures, drawings, and sculptures where the bidding is almost all by or on behalf of men; a female nude will always fetch a much higher price than a male nude of approximately the same quality.

The attitude of women, what they feel and think in the privacy of their own minds, is just as difficult to determine in regard to the male nude as to the female. On the whole, social history indicates that the majority of women do not select their husbands because they consider them handsome of face or beautiful of body. We may, therefore, be tempted to deduce that the majority of women must be indifferent towards pictures of naked men. It does not follow, however, that a woman who, given the opportunity to choose between a well-built and handsome man and one who is ugly of face and of poor physique, rejects the handsome suitor does so because she is not responsive to his sexual attractions. When it comes to choosing a spouse many women may be more level headed than many men.

Other women, however, or even the same women in different circumstances, especially when they are very young, can fall romantically in love, to the point of infatuation, with men they know they will never marry, and probably never meet, except with an autograph album in their hands. From the late 19th century onwards, actors and singers have been 'popular idols' and, while women no doubt feel released from inhibitions by the fact that a whole wave of erotic enthusiasm is public and millions participate in it, no one could seriously argue, in view of the cult of Rudolf Valentino in the 1920s, or the cult of the four singers and guitarists of the present day known as The Beatles, that women are by nature indifferent to masculine good looks. There is, however, one important distinction to be noted: women do not seem to wish their 'idols' to exhibit themselves, on stage or screen, as near to naked as the censor will allow. At least, the social changes of the 20th century, revolutionary as they are, have not created any strong feminine demand, in art or in entertainment, for male nudes.

This leads to two further considerations. Quite a number of pictures and drawings and sculptures which must be technically classified as nudes are, in intention and in effect, quite different from what is commonly meant by a nude. In these, the fact that a body or bodies are shown naked is subordinated to, and often transcended by, qualities that arouse intense and highly serious emotions, qualities that in the 18th century were often gathered together under the philosophical term, the Sublime. Michelangelo's huge 'David', in gleaming white marble, at the Gallery of the Accademia in Florence, is universally acknowledged as the outstanding example of the nude male sublime, not only by the artist's skill but by something majestic in the concept. Again, in religious art, at least in Western Christian art, the nude is often reduced to a comparatively minor element in the composition by other influences. The figure of Jesus crucified or taken down from the Cross is by tradition — quite possibly a tradition deriving from historical fact — shown naked except for a loin cloth. Such depictions, and others dealing with martyrdoms, are not nudes in the ordinary sense and have therefore been excluded from this survey.

The second consideration, which arises from the perceptible variations in response to the nude in men and in women, is the effect this may have upon the interest taken by the artist, and by those who appreciate works of art, in the human face. From a physiological — indeed from any scientific — point of view, the face is merely the front of the head, and the head is a kind of upward extension of the trunk, the brain as it were sprouting out of the spinal cord and being enclosed in a protective ball of bone called the skull. Because of the upright posture achieved by man, the head is the topmost, instead of the foremost, part of the body, and the face as a whole is directed towards the horizon instead of partly to the ground. The pineal gland is connected to the floor of the brain at its mid-line, and has been considered to be a vestigial third eye.

It is even said that some people, presumably through these vestiges, are sensitive to light directed on to the top of the head and, when they are blindfolded, can report accurately when such a light is switched on and off. This is held to indicate that among our more distant ancestors was a lizard or lizard-like creature, moving on four feet, with a single eye fixed forward like the headlamp on a motor cycle. Surviving bones and fossils from the remote past do not tell us as much as we might wish about the way the flesh was draped upon them, but it seems highly probable that, over long prehistoric ages, the human face, to conform with the needs of the upright bodily posture, not only changed the angle of the facial plane but rearranged the comparative sizes and placings of the features. For example, a hairless forehead was inserted between the eyebrows — themselves diminishing in size and thickness — and the carpet of hair covering the crown of the head. This happened, presumably, as the skull was enlarged, generation after generation, to accommodate a larger brain.

Another difference between the faces of prehistoric men so far as they can be hypothetically reconstructed and modern human faces is also worth noting. Prehistoric faces ended more or less at the mouth, with only a small chin hidden under and behind it: in other words, the lower, movable jaw was not comparable in size or prominence with the upper jaw. The jutting chin, so often equated with strength of will and an heroic character, is a comparatively modern development and may be due principally to the change in diet when human beings took to meat instead of living on fruits, roots, and leaves.

The face is of great importance in all human communications. It is situated in the most noticeable part of the whole body, and in it are gathered together the chief organs of the senses. Only the sense of touch has its outposts spread over the whole surface of the body — the skin can, in fact, be regarded as a sense organ and the most extensive of all. What we hear, what we see, what we smell, what we taste we experience through some part of our face and, because the face is situated so close to the brain, the transmission of messages along the appropriate nerves could hardly be more instantaneous. By looking at a person's face we often can come very close to perceiving what he is experiencing, moment by moment, because of tiny modifications of the facial expression. These modifications, which, in various degrees, can be controlled, simulated, and suppressed, are due partly to eye movements and variations in the focussing of the eyes and partly to infinitesimal modulations of the surface texture of the mouth and the cheeks adjacent to the mouth, controlled by a complex of tiny muscles. These muscles of facial expression are controlled by the facial nerve. It is a tenable theory that the reason the human face is capable of such a variety of expressions is that the nerves and muscles of the face are evolutionary leftovers from some very remote and fishlike ancestor. Similarly, human lips, teeth, and tongue — instruments for eating and drinking — have in the course of time been adapted to produce controlled, intelligible, and systematic sounds which, as language, provide the technique not only for all communication but for all thinking above the most primitive level. It is reasonable, indeed logical, therefore, that costume, however much it varies from time to time and from place to place, should usually contrive not only to leave the face uncovered but to give it a special emphasis. The exceptions to this rule are not accidental but designed for particular and exceptional purposes. When men cover their faces, all but the eyes, it may be to protect the face against injury, as with mediaeval helmets and 20th-century 'respirators' worn to nullify poison gas. Or the face may be hidden behind a veil or a scarf to keep out wind, snow, or sand. In the past, masks have been used to create mystery and instil awe, symbolically by the ancient Greeks for theatrical impersonation, and — in quite small forms — at Venetian balls held in Venice or elsewhere, to make identification difficult rather than impossible. Eye-masks of this kind, bands of cloth about two inches deep with holes cut for the wearer to see through, were traditionally worn by highwaymen of the 18th century when robbing stage coaches, and in the next century by burglars, such as the fictitious Bill Sikes and the real-life Charley Peace. Veils worn by women are of two kinds: those intended, by interposing an ornamental network, merely to make the face look more beautiful and those worn for religious reasons, by Moslem women and by certain orders of nuns, to prevent the face from being seen by men. These cover the lower part of the face, below the eyes — the very part left uncovered by the masks worn by Venetian gallants, highwaymen, and burglars.

The use of masks and veils, in fact, only emphasizes the importance we all attach to the face as an index to personality. We can gather a great deal from a voice and from what a voice says, and we can supplement this with knowledge of actions and of words committed to paper, but something vital is missing from our knowledge of a man or woman if we do not know what sort of face he or she has. Sometimes, with men, a great deal of the face is obscured by beard and moustache, and, if the mouth is also concealed behind hair, all the facial evidence is concentrated into the eyes and the region immediately around the eyes. It is perhaps for this reason that an excessive amount of hair on the face is regarded sometimes with reverence, sometimes with resentment and even ridicule; so much concealment, it is felt, would be proper only in men of great saintliness or majesty, and if the owner of the beard falls in his behaviour below such high standards, he may come in for severe criticism.

It is not only women who use costume to make themselves beautiful in the eyes of others. The record of history, as well as the customs of more primitive peoples of the present day, shows that men are more likely to dress colourfully and expensively than women. It is possible that this tendency could be interpreted as a sign of modesty and that the ostrich feathers on the helmet, the puffed-out velvet breeches, the bright satin doublets, the silver and gold buttons, and the flowered waistcoats with which at different periods men have adorned themselves were merely devices to distract attention from the face, but the argument is a rather specious one. On the whole, women seem to be more honest than men in this respect and readier to acknowledge their own vanity and enslavement to fashion. Fashion supplies the fickleness of human nature with an excuse for getting rid of clothing long before it is worn out, but — very much to the advantage of tailors, dressmakers, designers, and shopkeepers — it no sooner produces a successful 'novelty' than success makes the new style so popular that it quickly ceases to be a 'novelty'. Thus, while it is true that fashion does sometimes attempt to distract attention from the face towards what psychologists call one of the 'erotogenic zones' of the body, the attempt inevitably fails. When (as in the late 16th century) every woman pads out her dress over her hip bones until she looks as though she had a second pair of shoulders just below the level of her waist, when all fashionable breasts are covered only by transparent muslin (as in Paris under the Directoire), or when (as in the 1960s) all skirts are tight and shorter than any Scotsman would wear a kilt, the emphasis dictated by fashion loses all its force through repetition. Some legs, some arms, some bosoms are better shaped and better coloured than others, but the fact is that one pair of hips, padded or not; one pair of breasts, visible or not; and one pair of knees does not differ from another pair half so strikingly or so interestingly as one face from another face. Clothing, therefore, despite the vagaries of fashion, always tends to isolate the face and thereby to enhance its value as an element in the total appearance. The primary purpose of clothing is protective, against the weather, and not only in cold climates; it is also used in those hot countries where forests do not provide shadow from the glare of the sun. Clothing may cover every inch of the body except the face, and when custom and convention impose a uniformity, as in modern armed forces and as in late-19th-century dress for men, almost the whole individuality seems to be concentrated in the face. This is the tendency of costume taken to an extreme. If we now consider the other extreme, the nude, as it has been recorded by artists at various historical periods, we realize that the face depicted on canvas or wood panel, on plastered wall or paper, in bronze or stone competes for attention against the remainder of the body as it rarely has to do in real life. The competition would be severe enough — for the size of the remainder of the body is much greater than that of the head — if the nakedness of other

2

people were something to which everyday life accustomed us, but, even in the middle of the 20th century, this is not so. Anyone naked, or nearly naked, except at a bathing place, constitutes an unusual sight. Nakedness, therefore, has a great advantage over costume in attracting attention. It is true that the nude in art is accepted easily enough by most people, because social convention has established its harmlessness and its prestige, but within that convention the emphasis is on 'the body' — by which we mean not the whole body but the body from the shoulders down.

This usage reveals quite a lot about the way our minds work. Much of our thinking, and our unconscious formulation of concepts and judgments, is done by oscillations and vibrations between two opposites. It is as if the polarity — the magnetic field — between 'north' and 'south' had parallels in our minds, as if our mental activity were largely dependent on the existence of pairs of opposites. Thus a great deal of religious and ethical discussion is something like a magnetic field between concepts of 'material' and 'spiritual' values, each being defined (to some degree at least) as the opposite of the other. This polarisation of ideas, this habit of creating a paired-off antithesis of opposites, good and evil, civilized and barbaric, romantic and classic — or romantic and realist — may be intrinsic in the human mind, possibly because our senses, from which the mind is fed, supply us with similar ranges of experience, from black to white, from rough to smooth, from sharp to sweet.

There is an obvious and convenient contrast between complete nakedness and complete costuming in which only the face is visible; and, because our minds work, not always precisely and not always consciously, by such technical devices as symbolism and association it is possible that, for all of us at times and for some of us all the time, the idea of nakedness automatically brings up ideas of evil, or sexuality or materialism, ideas that draw their power and definition largely by contrast with ideas of good, asceticism or spirituality. If this is so, many of us, probably without suspecting it, may have in our minds as permanent furniture a contrast between the head, of which the face is the important visible part, and the rest of the body, something like the theological contrast between flesh and spirit. The body may even come to symbolize 'the world', that aspect of existence concerned with gratifying the physical appetites and which has, as its

19

contrasting opposite, God as a spiritual being not perceptible through the senses at all. When this happens the body is likely to be thought of as a thing of shame and wrapped in form-concealing draperies, while the face, symbolizing the seat of reason and morality, is conceived as something formalized to the point of abstraction, a rendering of a lofty idea rather than a part of the body. Because of such polarities in our minds, we may expect the faces of nudes in art to make a different effect than the faces of persons fully clad, either realistically, in portraiture, or in some imaginary composition. For the draughtsman or the sculptor, the problem is largely one of proportion and emphasis. He has to decide, or to discover in the course of experiment, whether the head is to be the focussing point of interest in his composition or is to be subordinated to some other part of the body, how much of the face he will make visible and how its modelling should be rendered. For the painter there are added to these problems other problems concerning colour and tone. The same face is going to take on a different appearance in juxtaposition to expanses of bare skin from the appearance it has emerging from arrangements of wool, cotton, linen, silk, or fur.

Some artists have evaded the whole problem of matching the face to the nude body by omitting it altogether, or turning it away from view, or indicating it only sketchily. Such omissions are justified sometimes on the ground that a face can only distract from the aesthetic effect of a nude body, or that all female nudes are, to one degree or another, erotic; and eroticism should be concerned with breasts and thighs and other attributes which arouse desire the more strongly if the personality is negligible. This may have been, more often than not, the attitude of Degas, who so often contrived, not only in his nudes but in his studies of ballet girls and washerwomen, to have the face turned away or thrown into heavy shadow, as if to proclaim that he was interested in his models merely as shapes and colours and outlines, not at all as human beings.

chapter 3

Scholars in the 18th century, despite their almost excessive reverence for Greek and Roman art and literature, were in the habit of referring to the whole of the remote past under the hold-all name of Antiquity. What happened before the Homeric Age and after the disruption of the Roman Empire seemed obscure and of small importance. Nowadays the whole concept of past time has been stretched, by geology and physics and chemistry as well as by archaeology, and vast quantities of ascertained, hypothetical, or deduced facts have been added to our knowledge of primitive human communities living tens of thousands of years ago. We have also learned a great deal about early civilizations — such as the Cretan, the Mycenaean, the Hittite, the Celtic, the Etruscan — that within living memory were so vaguely known that they seemed almost mythical. There is at present almost a surfeit of information, and the general philosophy that is, at any period, common to well-educated people can hardly yet be said to have adapted itself adequately. For example, reproductions of coloured drawings found in caves, in what is now Spain and France, are familiar to most of us, and we know, in general terms, that they were done by 'cave men' 10,000 years or more ago. What is not so easy to appreciate is that in conception, in design, and in execution these cave drawings are 'advanced'. For artistic quality they may be thought to surpass the finest products of many subsequent ages. For draughtsmanship they were unmatched in the West except by certain Greek vase paintings — where the convention is not dissimilar — until the Italian Renaissance brought in the great modern age of drawing and painting.

It would therefore be grossly misleading to regard the history of art as a record of steady progress, with new technical improvements being added from time to time, and with variety arising chiefly from historical changes in costume, architecture, manufactured goods, and social habits. It is not possible to establish fixed standards of aesthetic value that can be checked by measurements and other observations. The comfortable certitudes of science are not valid in art. Everything goes by what people like — and by what people can be persuaded to like. The most legitimate means of persuasion is by increasing understanding. Uniformity of taste and opinion is not to be expected and is hardly desirable. Tastes and opinions differ not only among contemporaries, and not only from one period to another, but in the preferences two periods may show among works of art surviving from still earlier times. No sooner was Botticelli dead than Italian taste, and international taste so far as it then existed, lost interest in him. In the 17th, the 18th, and the greater part of the 19th century the 'Primavera' and 'The Birth of Venus', which everybody now finds enchanting, were regarded as very minor and unexciting works by a quite obscure painter. Towards the end of the 18th century the English reverence for Raphael — which was to be revived, too late, by the Victorians — had so far weakened that a rich man travelling in Italy and finding an opportunity to buy either a Raphael or a Guido Reni would inevitably choose the Reni. The agents and commissioners who, a little later, accompanied the French armies invading various parts of Europe to seize valuable paintings, in the name first of the French Republique, later of the Napoleonic Empire, often exhibited similar preferences which today seem inexplicable.

Of the two major styles of Greek art, which can be given the summary names of the Archaic and the Classic, the Classic style — the later of the two — was obviously preferred by the Romans who, as they absorbed the Greek states into their Empire, shipped vases and sculpture in great quantities to Rome. This may have been because the earlier style seemed comparatively unskilful, incapable of simulating in stone the free, lissom movements of arms and legs, or the delicate folding of fine, almost transparent fabrics over human flesh, such as can be seen in the exquisite relief, preserved in Rome, known as the Ludovisi Throne. The Archaic style was limited and inexpressive, but the forms it produced, after more than 2000 years of disfavour, approximate more closely the prevailing taste of the 20th century than those of the Classic style. The taste of to-day, however, is very much in reaction against the taste, which prevailed until the end of the 19th century, for styles deriving from the Italian Renaissance, especially from Raphael and Michelangelo. Those styles, as the name Renaissance implies, were themselves derived — often through Roman copies and imitations — from the Classic style of Greece.

One of the strongest temptations besetting those who write art history is to express opinions and interpretations as if they were matters of acknowledged fact. Anyone may now and then commit such an unintended deception, but if it becomes a habit, it is a vice. Impressive statements about what went on in the minds of artists, long since dead, of whom we know practically nothing, should always be sceptically received. Speculations on such subjects is an exercise of the imagination, which may be illuminating, but if it is put forward with authority as factual, it is a lie. The first thing therefore to be made clear about the art of Ancient Greece, of both the Archaic and Classic periods, is that we have remarkably little indisputable information about it. No paintings at all have survived, except those that decorate vases and are, in effect, monochrome or two-colour drawings. The architecture consists of ruins. The names of some of the leading Greek sculptors — Pheidias, Myron, Praxiteles, Scopas, and others — are known, but there is no certain means of attributing particular works to any one of them. Almost all the sculpture that survives is damaged.

There is evidence that some figure sculpture was painted. Perhaps all Greek sculpture except figures done partly in gold, partly in ivory, was painted; perhaps the paint was renewed at intervals. Traces of pigment remain on some pieces. But our traditional idea of 'Greek sculpture' as carvings in gleaming white marble is almost certainly a false one. It is possible that a citizen of Athens, miraculously restored to life and set down in front of the Medici Venus or the Apollo Belvedere — after he had solved a scholar-vexing problem and told us whether or not they are Roman copies of Greek originals — would express astonishment and shock; what would shock him would be not the nudity of the figures but the fact that they consist of bare marble with no decent covering of paint.

It seems reasonable to conclude that, as the Greeks balanced the solemn tragedies of their theatre with ribald farces, the small figures of grotesque old men and women, often caricatures, often in vulgar poses, that have survived with thousands of other terracottas, supply, as it were, the other extreme — the opposite pole to the heroic, athletic figures of gods, goddesses, warriors, matrons, high-born maidens, and aged councillors (Roman as well as Greek) which, together with the great buildings they were designed to decorate, make up the idea of classic art most of us carry in our minds. There is another contrast to be noted. For many people, classic art, including the Greek, might also be called 'romantic' because it arouses pleasurable emotions and by doing so affords relief from the pettiness, the commonplace quality, of everyday life. This is a valid observation but a confusing one, and the confusion arises from the different functions we make the word 'romantic' perform. We do this because it is in the nature of our minds to seek an opposite for almost every idea we have.

The globe we live on is tilted between magnetic north and magnetic south and spins us perpetually from night to day and back again, so it is hardly surprising that our thoughts tend to establish such polarities. The tendency is so much part of ourselves that we are hardly aware of it, and very often we muddle one polarity with another. When the word 'classic' is used to indicate orderliness, restraint, and pre-calculated proportions strictly adhered to, the word 'romantic' is a convenient name for antithetical qualities such as a haphazard appearance, an extravagant manner, and designs dependent on improvisation. 'Romantic', however, by a later, but perhaps commoner, usage, serves also to indicate qualities that are the opposite of 'realistic' or 'naturalistic'. In this sense the word 'romantic' cannot be validly used of Greek Classic art because an outstanding quality of that art is that it is naturalistic. It represents people and things with little or no departure from reality. Moreover, it is probable that the Greeks themselves valued their classic sculpture largely because it seemed to them to represent its subjects faithfully. The Romans, who collected Greek sculpture, coins, and vases as art treasures — estimable both as things of beauty and as valuables — and whose own art closely followed Greek models, seem to have held similar views. So did the scholars and artists of the Italian Renaissance. The function of art was to imitate or counterfeit natural appearances, to "hold the mirror up to Nature," as Hamlet says, admonishing the actors he considers to be too extravagant in gesture and speech. Truthful representation was in fact the declared aim and ideal of most art from the 5th century B.C. to the 5th century A.D. and from the 15th century to the end of the 19th. Whether European art has always conformed to its professed intentions is another question altogether.

Common sense, as well as the existence of portrait busts and grotesque or deformed figures, indicates that not all Greeks were beautiful; we may therefore conclude that such representations as the 'Venus de Milo' are projections of an ideal of feminine beauty. The 'Venus de Milo' takes its name from the island where it was discovered in 1820. At that time Melos belonged to Turkey, and only with difficulty, and perhaps some bribery, did the French Ambassador get the figure shipped to France. When it reached the Louvre, the marble Venus was acclaimed as a masterpiece by Praxiteles but was not shown to the general public for more than 60 years. The reason may have been scholarly shame, for some observers believe that when part of the plinth was recovered from Melos it bore an inscription declaring that the sculpture was the work of "Agesandros, son of Menides of Antioch-in-Meander". This meant that the experts had not only given the credit to the wrong sculptor but had erred by nearly 200 years in dating it, and — most humiliating of all — had put the name of a great master on the handiwork of an obscure provincial. The general public might retort that the marble figure is no more and no less beautiful whomever it is attributed to, and this is in effect what visitors to the Louvre have been saying ever since. The 'Venus de Milo', without arms, remains the most famous of all sculptures. The plinth with the tell-tale inscription has long been lost, and there is a good reason to believe that when the statue was first discovered the two arms, although broken off, were present in the underground shrine. They have also disappeared. The chip knocked off during the trip to Tokyo in 1964, however, has presumably been replaced. It has sometimes been argued that the figure represents not the goddess of love but a deity peculiar to Melos. The convention of depicting the female body naked above the waist, however, with the clothes draped around the legs and just about to slip off is, for obvious reasons, usually considered to be a way of denoting that the sculpture represents Aphrodite. We have no certain indication of the women from whom such sculptures were derived, although there is a story that the model for the statue of Aphrodite by Praxiteles, erected at Cnidus, was a famous courtesan called Phryne. Another story has it that Phryne once secured an acquittal in a court of law by tearing open her dress and exhibiting her breasts to the judges. The 'Cnidian Venus', however, is known only through a Roman copy, and we cannot identify even two or three depictions of the same model by three different artists and make comparisons to guess what she looked like in real life. What we can do is to see with our own eyes that there are, living in Greece and in Italy and in other Mediterranean countries today, young women who in face as well as in physique remind us of goddesses and nymphs carved — from the evidence of the sculptor's eyes as well as from his imagination — more than 2000 years ago. For the taste of Northern peoples, and for the taste of the present century, the Greek Classic ideal, despite its beauty, may not be beyond criticism: the torso may be thought too broad and too thick, especially at the waist, and the face lacking in individual character and in expressiveness. Symmetry — a predetermined proportion of the parts to the whole and an overall effect of balance and stability — was considered an essential of beauty, and the Hellenes of the 5th and 4th centuries B.C. may have looked at sculpture, as at architecture, with a mathematical and analytic particularity which few nowadays, even among professed art lovers, could achieve. The Greeks were justified in so far as their classic style served as the criterion of art for the Romans and for the Renaissance Italians, and their ideal of human beauty, though there have been fashions and doctrines to flout it, is still powerful in all our minds.

The Classic style was in its time new, modern, experimental, innovating. It distinguished Greece from such nearby countries as Egypt, Persia, and Assyria and made her European rather than Oriental in art. It might be said that what Myron, Pheidias, Praxiteles, and others did was to take the monumental stiffness out of the bulky arms and legs, and the sacklike torsos of Archaic sculptures, and wipe the enigmatic, wedge-shaped smile off the bland, impersonal faces. On many people today, the enigmatic smile — which may have arisen merely as a convention suitable for sculptors of limited skill, unable to chip deep without splitting the stone — and the too obviously monolithic poses exercise a special charm, much as the naïveté of modern 'primitives' such as the Douanier Rousseau and Chagall, whether it is genuine or a self-conscious affectation, appeals to many people. The attraction lies, surely, in novelty, and what is novel for us in the 20th century about archaic Greek sculpture is that it contradicts most of the principles of the Classic style. If things had gone the other way — if the Archaic style had followed and supplanted the Classic and had deeply influenced later artists — the same people who now overpraise such figures as the 'Apollo of Tenea' (Plate 3) might instead be rhapsodizing over the Venus de Milo as 'strange', 'mysterious', and 'enigmatic'.

It is difficult, however, to conceive any circumstances short of cataclysmic in which the Archaic style could have followed the Classic. Heavily monumental figure sculpture has been made at different times in all sorts of places from Bangkok and Easter Island to any back garden where children slap together a snow man for Christmas, and nowhere has it evolved into anything subtle, various, and expressive without changing its principles and being transformed beyond recognition. In brief, the Archaic style was incapable of much development. The likeliest reason why the Classic style triumphed was that some sculptors became experimental and, improving their skill, discovered new ways of using mallet and chisel and punch, and, excited by the discoveries, began to make, for the first time, free-standing figures in a variety of poses, with air and light between limbs and body, convincing representations of reality, natural yet with a grace excelling the transient graces of Nature.

In 5th- and 4th-century sculptures of goddesses, the whole frontal aspect of the head, mainly occupied by the face, describes an outline that is sometimes called the classic oval. This is not quite a geometric oval; it is rather broader in the upper part, at the level of the eyes, than in the lower part. It is evenly balanced between one side and the other, and the surface is plump, the convexities more noticeable than the tiny concavities at the corners of the mouth, under the lower lip, and around the eyes. Because the mouth is richly curved there is thus over the whole face a complex interplay of curved surfaces in three dimensions. A similar interplay of light and shade varies with the direction and strength of the light and with the position of the viewer. The characteristic masculine face, as in the Apollo Belvedere and the Hermes from Olympia, is just as full of interacting surface curves. The classic oval outline in men's faces, however, is apt to become angular where the lower jaw bone joins the upper beneath the ears, and the chin is often narrower though still rounded out into a boss. To a 20th-century critic there are two disconcerting characteristics observable in such faces, characteristics at odds with our own ideals of masculine beauty: both the effervescences of curls over the top of the head and the dimples on the chin and beside the mouth remind us of small babies. Is has to be admitted, however, that the dimples and curls, because of the infantile associations, actually may increase the attraction such faces have for women. At least three film stars of recent years have owed part of their success to faces reminiscent of the Greek classic ideal: the late Clark Gable, Kirk Douglas, and — outstandingly — Victor Mature.

Feminine faces with the classic oval shape have been considered beautiful by so many generations all over the civilized world that it is easier to reject them than to criticize them in detail. They are perfect — using the word in the sense of faultless —examples of facial symmetry, and it is no doubt their look of faultlessness that provokes some people into declaring they are dull

3

Ludovico Cordi, called il Cigoli (1559–1613), Narcissus, Paris, The Louvre.

or even positively displeasing. The classic oval face inevitably looks serene, and serene may be not far from placid. If to the symmetric proportions of the face there is added clear and even colouring, beautiful hair, and brilliant eyes, the effect can be quite overwhelming. This effect may, however, diminish with day-by-day repetition, while faces less impressive at first sight may become more interesting — and so more beautiful — under close and repeated scrutiny. What people of a romantic disposition require in a face before they admit it is beautiful is, probably, a hint of strangeness, something unforeseen, something to disturb and diversify the carefully disposed symmetries. Viewed from one side, the classic oval face, in both masculine and feminine versions, sometimes — though not always — discloses such a pleasantly surprising quality in the once famous 'Grecian profile' of the upper half of the face. This has no indentation above the nose but makes a single unbroken line from the top of the forehead to the tip of the nose. It is perhaps a deficiency in the Greek classic ideal that the 'Grecian profile' is completely wasted from the front view.

It is uncertain whether the Greeks of the Classic period considered that different kinds of faces, or different ways of rendering the face, would be appropriate according to whether the body was clothed or naked. Time, weather, war, and other depredations have seen to it that while we have large numbers of sculptured torsos (most with arms and hands broken off, many without legs also), and large numbers of sculptured heads (most of them battered), it is a matter of opinion which heads came from which bodies. There is, however, little reason to suppose that the Greeks were able to foresee the rise of Christianity and its periodic bouts of puritanic warfare against "the flesh", and it is unlikely that their paganism was so self-conscious as to make their art a celebration of what Mr. Eric Newton has called "pride in the body". The pride was no doubt there but taken for granted. The antithesis, the contradictory idea of the body as something to be distrusted and subjected, had not yet made its mark on history. It is a matter of speculation, but it would at least be a tenable argument, that what Greek sculptors took greatest pride in was their skill and that they considered their skill was more fully exercised in rendering the cling and fall and ripple of fine-textured cloths, as in the 'Ludovisi Throne', over the human body than in depicting the body bare. It is notable that the Venus de Milo itself, probably the most celebrated of all nude sculptures, shows the goddess clothed from the waist down and for its effect depends a good deal on the contrast between the surfaces of bare flesh and woven cloth. The little-known sculptor of the island of Melos seems to have worked on the

principle — which many later artists have relied on — that a body which is partly clothed can be made to appear far more nude than a body completely devoid of covering.

chapter 4

It would be untrue to say that Roman art, during its most active period, from the 2nd century B.C. to the 4th century A.D., made no improvements or advances on the Greek achievement, but in general Roman sculpture, like Roman architecture, looks derivative, reminiscent, and often openly imitative of the Greek. It was perhaps most successful in the portrait bust — one enormous specimen, 10 times larger than life, survives in Rome, set into the old city wall near the Pincio Gardens and dominating the traffic bound for the Via Vittoria Veneto — and least successful with nude or semi-nude sculpture. What for modern taste is both stimulating and interesting in Roman art is the wall painting. Murals — they are not frescoes, brushed into wet plaster, but pictures done with a waxen or oily medium — that survive in the Naples Museum and elsewhere belong to the Roman decadence, when the Romans were deep under the spell of Greek art, and at one remove they tell us something of what Greek painting of the classical period, itself all destroyed, may have been like. They also show us that later Italian painting, much of it done in true fresco, took up and revived a decorative yet naturalistic tradition long forgotten and apparently broken. The English word *grotesque,* as well as the Italian *grottesco* (meaning a fanciful decoration often including vegetation and real or imaginary creatures among the ornamental scrolls) is derived from the *grottoes,* hollow places of all kinds, discovered as ruins. They began to be excavated early in the 16th century.

Much of Ancient Rome, including the Forum, was buried under accretions of earth and rubbish in the centuries after the barbarian invasions and the breakup of the Empire. The burial was literal enough: the ground level rose year by year. It was also unconsciously symbolical, for if the Greeks founded a European civilisation by resisting the force and the legendary luxuries of the Orient, the Romans, who saw themselves as the rightful heirs to the Greeks, were in their turn subordinated by an Oriental civilization, centred on Constantinople or Byzantium, which called itself Roman although many have regarded it as Greek. The Byzantine style in sculpture and painting and mosaic picture-making is widely different from the Greek classic style. It exercised an immense influence on the art of various states in the un-united country called Italy and, through Italy, on the rest of Europe. It is commemorated in great Romanesque churches — the name indicates the claim of Byzantium to have replaced Rome — in Ravenna and Milan. A little later the Venetians imported a still more Oriental kind of architecture — although it derived from Greeks working to please Turkish masters — when they built the cathedral of St. Mark, close to the lagoon whence their trading ships sailed, and decorated it with Byzantine mosaics, prancing horses cast in Corinthian bronze and a cluster of pointed golden domes.

The combination of barbarian raids, the breakdown of central government, and the rise of Byzantium was disastrous for the pictorial arts in Italy. The nude ceased to be. The Byzantine style had no use for it, for the style had reverted to a pseudo-monolithic treatment of the human figure: arms rarely lifted away from the sides and legs hardly ever separated as far as to undertake a single timid step. The body was always covered, heavily and formally cloaked in concealing robes. Faces were devoid of personal characteristics, as well as delicate variations of modelling, and were made into diagrams of crudely drawn black lines. The Byzantine style, which is primarily an architectural style, has its own virtues and is highly appreciated by some people, but its abstract simplifications were hostile to the development of interest in the human body and the human face as subjects for art.

The peoples of northern and western Europe, not all of them settled on the far side of the Alps from Italy, were peoples of whom we still know little: the Goths and Vandals, the Celts and others — like the Gauls, the Belgae, the Picts, the Cymrae, the Britons — who spoke Celtic languages, as well as nations or tribes called Germanic or Teutonic. They furnish from among them, how or why we do not fully understand, the component elements of the style — prevalent from the 12th century to the 15th — that is variously subdivided into Gothic, Norman, Perpendicular, Early English, and so on, but here is most conveniently summed up as Mediaeval. It is associated in architecture with narrow shapes, vertical or in ground plan, pointed arches, spires, flying buttresses, and gargoyles. The Mediaeval style can be seen in Italy itself (where the traditional shape for churches is that of the Greek temple and the Greek basilica) in the cathedrals of Milan and Orvieto. The Mediaeval style was much more favourable than the Byzantine to the pictorial arts, and the Church became the patron of painters and sculptors who were ranked as artisans — skilled labour. Neither independent artists nor profane art — that is to say, non-ecclesiastical art — can truly be said to have yet come into existence.

The verticals of Mediaeval architecture imposed a tendency to elongation on tombstone figures and on the carved figures of saints in niches; both were normally clothed and designed to move the onlooker to spiritual reverence rather than to admiration for physical beauty. In relief carvings, in the brightly coloured plates of illuminated books, and in a few altar pieces of the Middle Ages nude figures occur, but they are either figures of Christ on the cross, of saints suffering martyrdom, or of Adam and Eve. Adam and Eve, yielding to the serpentine Tempter or being banished from Paradise, were not required to be presented as attractive to the senses, and had an artist sought to depict them so it is likely that his work would have been rejected by his churchmen patrons and perhaps destroyed. As late as 1781, Joseph II — what is now Belgium was then part of the Austrian Empire — professed to be shocked by the nudity of the Adam and Eve on two side panels of the famous Van Eyck altarpiece in Ghent, where they were only two among quite a multitude of figures, all the rest of which were fully clothed. On the Emperor's orders the Adam and Eve panels were removed from the altarpiece and stored away out of sight. Thirteen years later they were confiscated by the commissioners who accompanied the French armies. They did not return to Brussels till 1815, after Waterloo.

Even when the Mediaeval period was being overlapped by the Early Renaissance and the painters of the Low Countries — no others then had the knowledge and skill — began to depict the nude with a brilliance, a smoothness of surface and a detailed illusionism made possible by the use of oil paints, their subjects were still Adam and Eve and, so far from celebrating the pride of the body, the primordial pair usually exhibit a distressing combination of bony limbs and pot belly. Such sculptures as the Mary Magdalene by Erhart (Plate 15), and the 'Eve' by Antonio Rizzo at the Ducal Palace in Venice often have a strong emotional effect. Even in the Memlinc at Vienna (where Adam and Eve are separated on complementary panels), the Van Eyck that shocked Joseph II (where on separate panels Adam and Eve turn away from each other), and the Hugo van der Goes at Vienna (where they share the same small picture with the fruit-laden Tree and a Tempter more like a lizard than a snake), the nudity is pitiful rather than alluring. These are all 15th-century paintings (strictly speaking Renaissance paintings), but in them the Middle Ages can be seen dying hard and grimly. It is not, however, only in their mastery of the oil-laden brush, often creating a crisp illusion of colourful reality hardly to be matched by photography, that these Northern paintings seem to belong less to the Middle Ages than to modern times. The faces, commonplace in themselves, are startling in work done so early. They are the faces not of types but of individual persons; they are faces we could remember and identify again. They might almost be described as portraits clapped, a little incongruously, on to naked bodies.

chapter 5

The idea of the Renaissance is so fundamental to our thinking, and to the assumptions from which our thinking proceeds, that the outlines of its complicated history can be taken as part of a common knowledge. Not all scholars and commentators are agreed, though, about the scope and the duration of the Renaissance in the pictorial arts. Here it will be regarded as occurring chiefly in 15th-century Italy — coming to its climax early in the 16th century with the major works of Michelangelo, Raphael, and others in a style and period often called the High Renaissance; having a delayed effect in other countries; and being overtaken from about 1520 by an unorganized movement or style to which in our own time the name of Mannerism has been given.

Just as in the emergence of the Greek Classic style in sculpture an improved technique must have been decisive, so the discovery of a superior kind of refined oil, which would make a more practicable mixture with ground-earth pigments, was crucial to the Renaissance development of painting. In the end, oils triumphed everywhere over the rival media of egg yolk or egg white (tempera) and lime water (fresco), so much so that the very word 'painting' has come to mean 'painting in oil colours'. The reason was that with oil colours it became possible to alternate impasto with thin glazes and even to put one on top of the other, to use brushes more delicately and variously, and in general to represent all kinds of things — from leaves and flowers to human faces and human bodies — more vividly and more convincingly.

The victory did not come with a single stroke. Oils were not welcomed everywhere; Michelangelo — who lived on till 1564 and, himself the greatest of the Renaissance artists, is the true founder of Mannerism — painted only in tempera and fresco. Oil colours, however, established new standards of lifelikeness. They set the pace; they showed the possibilities open once the Mediaeval restrictions on subject and treatment were set aside. What the original Renaissance, the Revival of Learning — of which the greater part now seems drearily academic — contributed to the Renaissance in the pictorial arts was figures: figures in action and, very often, nude figures involved in stories from Greek and Latin poems, history books, fables, myths, and legends.

The rich men with palaces and country villas to decorate — princes of the Church as well as princes by dynastic right, and merchant princes — created new visions and a widespread demand. For the first time in a thousand years, painters and sculptors were no longer confined to work for and in churches, abbeys, and monasteries. Paradoxically, however, the greatest of all Renaissance paintings were done on the spot in the Vatican: Michelangelo's elaborate decorations of the compartmented ceiling of the Sistine Chapel and Raphael's story-telling frescoes, generally called the Stanze. The paradox arises from the fact that the Vatican was a palazzo and the Pope was not only spiritual head of the Church but a temporal monarch; that is to say, a land-owning, power-wielding prince often in competition with others who called themselves King or Duke or Grand Duke.

Michelangelo had already made his name as a sculptor with a 'Bacchus' (now in the Bargello at Florence) which has an oddly pagan and decadent air, the poignantly Christian 'Pietà' (at St. Peter's), and the huge, heroic 'David' (now in the Accademia at Florence) which might well be taken as a challenge, and a successful one, to all the sculptors of Ancient Greece and Rome. He completed the 'David' four years before he began work on the Sistine Chapel ceiling, and that marble glorification of an ideal of nude masculine beauty must have been in his mind, as a superb conception superbly realized, while he prepared, by means of preliminary drawings — studies from the life, experimental composition sketches, and working cartoons — for the arduous labour of painting every inch of the ceiling himself as he sprawled, strained, and stretched on scaffolding erected just below the ceiling. The marble 'David' is close kin to the painted 'Adam' who, reclining with raised knee and one arm outstretched, is almost as majestic as the bearded God the Father flying and floating creatively across the surface of the earth. It is sometimes said that Michelangelo's young women are often adaptations from his drawings of young men, and that, although the Sistine ceiling represents many Old Testament prophets and leaders, the installation — at the head of columns and in other lofty and significant places — of Sibyls and even more of the Ignudi (figures of handsome, athletic, and naked young men), makes the chapel ceiling, in effect, a Greek pantheon. If so, it is still a work of high seriousness and one charged with profound emotion. This is made all the clearer if it is compared with the two large ceiling paintings, each showing an assembly of the Gods, which Raphael provided, also in Rome, to illustrate the story of Cupid and Psyche.

Raphael, however, employed a number of assistants at the Villa Farnesina who may have made drawings and prepared cartoons as well as done most of the painting. According to Vasari, the reason Raphael neglected this work was that he was in love — with whom we do not know, despite all the guesses identifying the unknown mistress with the models for various portraits and Madonna pictures. A fair comparison between Raphael and Michelangelo, as painters, must take into account also Raphael's frescoes for the Stanze at the Vatican — a series of rather square and, by comparison with the Sistine Chapel, small and low-ceilinged rooms. Here Raphael provided allegorical compositions about philosophy and theology, and others that tell the stories of miraculous events: the release of St. Peter from prison by an angel, the Mass at Bolsena when the reigning Pope performed a miracle, and the expulsion of Heliodorus from the Temple.

If the comparison were competitive, to decide which is the greater of the two artists — their contemporaries took sides on this issue most vehemently — many other factors would need to be taken into account. For example, we should have to remember that Raphael died at the age of 37 while Michelangelo lived to be 89, and that Raphael habitually worked with and through many assistants — some of them highly gifted — while Michelangelo, like at least two other Florentines — Pontormo and Francesco Salviati — preferred to work alone. We should remember also that the Sistine Chapel ceiling is difficult to appreciate on the spot; it can hardly be seen as a whole without foreshortening of the more distant parts, and it can be viewed part by part only by straining the neck and shoulder muscles. By contrast, Raphael's Vatican frescoes can be viewed while one stands upright and at close range. This, however, means that Raphael's work, besides losing something of the effect lent to the Sistine ceiling by a lofty position overhead, may be, and often is, subjected to a more severe, inch-by-inch criticism.

Our minds seek out and enjoy contrasts, and it would be possible to express the development of modern art, to the end of the 19th century, as movements of attraction and repulsion towards and away from the ideals Raphael stood for or is believed to have stood for. Michelangelo does not lend himself so easily to such an interpretation of history. He can easily be made to establish a strong polarity as against Raphael, but if he himself is treated as the initial point of reference, an opposite pole is not always easy to define.

Raphael may be viewed as the great man of the High Renaissance, as the artist who epitomises it as a movement of reaction and emergence from the stiff, solid, gold-leaf conventions of the Primitives. Raphael is an excellent illustration of the Renaissance as a revival of the forgotten Graeco-Roman ideals of balance, proportions deriving from those of the presumed averages of the human figure, dignity combined with a total effect of repose and stability, and — in the face — the classic oval outline and a gamut of expres-

siveness no greater than from benevolence to serenity. In this sense he is a valid symbol or rather his Holy Family paintings, the 'Raphael Madonnas' so much revered and bought and sold at such high prices in the later part of the 19th century, constitute a valid symbol. It may be that one reason the Victorians overesteemed 'Raphael Madonnas' was that they could be reasonably sure the pictures were the work of the master's own and unaided hand. With frescoes and cartoons it is not always possible to say convincingly which parts are by Raphael and which by one of his assistants, each of whom, after the master's early death, made a brilliant career for himself. The authorship of some Raphael drawings is in dispute, and the influence of Raphael's way of using chalk or pen can be seen in the work not only of Perino del Vaga, Giulio Romano, Sebastiano Piombo, Giovanni Francesco Penni, and Timoteo Viti who worked under and with him, but in the drawings of Parmigianino and Salviati, and indeed of Rubens — who knew his work posthumously and only during visits to Rome. For most people's taste today, however, the Madonna pictures are not Raphael's greatest achievement; his importance depends rather on his frescoes in Roman churches and in the Vatican, and on his numerous drawings (including the huge and imposing cartoons, for tapestry weavers to follow) at the Victoria and Albert Museum in London. In many of these there are noticeable elements that seem to conflict with the classical ideal. In 'The Death of Ananias', for example, the dying man on the floor, the two men crouching over him, and the man on one knee who extends an arm in front of him make up a pattern of distorted cruciform shapes which, if the cartoon were by Rosso, would seem quite typical of Florentine Mannerism.

The 'Disputa', the 'Parnassus', and 'School of Athens' frescoes are rich in repose and symmetry: few of the faces have any very positive expression, and such incidental nudity as occurs has no discernible connection with sex. In these frescoes it is easy to discern that Raphael was once the pupil of Perugino and could produce work that was bound to please churchmen trained in the inherent logic of the Latin language and temperamentally inclined to a Horatian view of restraint. Even in these compositions, however, so carefully thought out and calculated that they are almost architectural, some of the groups, coherent in themselves, are made up of figures with little or no repose. The more dramatic frescoes, 'The Expulsion of Heliodorus', have themes that call for a different treatment and, while the greater part of the work on them was done after Raphael's rival, Michelangelo, had completed the Sistine Chapel ceiling in the same building, it is too easy to account for the difference by claiming that Raphael had captured a new and revolutionary concept of art or that he had himself become a Mannerist. Some art historians argue that it was the forcible temperament of Giulio Romano, his chief pupil and assistant, that supplied the Mannerist element in Raphael's work. Mr. Frederick Hartt, in his monograph on Giulio (Yale University Press, 1958), maintains that Giulio was encouraged, or at least allowed, by Raphael not only to carry out in fresco Raphael's designs but to supply his own, including some lifesize cartoons of single figures. This is to claim more for Giulio than many would concede. Recurrent in certain Raphael compositions is a type of young woman, plump of body and face and with round, full breasts, arms, and legs that almost thicken towards wrists and ankles. The Galatea and the Psyche at the Villa Farnesina belong to this type; and the shapeless arms, stretched upward, are prominent in 'The Fire in the Borgo'. The type may be the product of Giulio's hand, but hardly of his imagination, for it occurs in several mural decorations surviving from Pompeii and Herculaneum. It may represent a persistent Roman ideal of feminine beauty.

Although the three dramatic frescoes have more vigorous physical action, and although some of the faces express powerful emotions, the compositions as a whole are still 'Classical'; they are balanced, contained, and planned to counteract their own elements and to make the disruptive spend its visual force within the outer margins of the picture. In 'The Expulsion of Heliodorus', moreover, although at the left a man has climbed a pillar to see the better, and the right foreground is occupied by a mounted warrior making his horse rear above the sprawling figure of the looting Heliodorus, the major effect is three-dimensional, and the viewer's eye is led through recessions of arches into an illusionary depth where Pope Leo IV is seen intently praying at an altar. Raphael remains classical. He constructs a picture as if he were constructing a building of precisely shaped but inflexible, unaccommodating units.

chapter 6

The antithesis, the irreconcilable clash between a style and outlook we can for convenience call Classical or High Renaissance and a style and outlook we can call Mannerism, is authentic. This does not mean, however, that works of art, and still less the 16th-century artists who produced them, can all be neatly separated into two classes. It is true that Michelangelo, a man who took life hard and conceived it as a conflict, exemplifies a great deal though not all (not the elegance or attenuation of the human body, for example) of what came to be known as Mannerism.

But just as much as Raphael he bent his mind to the task of inducing the disruptive elements to cohere into an organized whole. There is, therefore, a sense in which Michelangelo should be regarded as a classical painter. In his sculpture — which was all carved, not modelled in clay to be afterwards cast in metal — he was classical to the point of creating, in the figures for the Medici Tombs, an overall effect of stability and repose that is still the ultimate criterion for any funeral statuary with recumbent figures. Some artists are perhaps outside this magnetic field altogether: Pisanello, Botticelli, and Filippino Lippi may be considered too early in time and style, but while some critics judge them as Late Gothic, others see the two Florentines, at least, as proto-Mannerists. Signorelli (Plates 13-14), and the Pollaiuoli, who with vigorous postures foreshadow Michelangelo's Sistine paintings, might also be called Mannerists before their time. But Pinturicchio, Massaccio, Mantegna, Leonardo himself, Fra Bartolomeo, Andrea del Sarto, and all the Venetians before Tintoretto and Veronese can reasonably be called, in general terms, 'Classical' painters.

The antithesis is there, between the coherent and the uneasy or actually explosive composition, between the face depicted as one part of the body and the face made to convey a message about what is going on, at the chosen moment, in the mind. Between the clothed body and the nude body, however, any antithesis is subdued or latent until about 1520, the time when Mannerism began to be more fashionable and more influential than the Classical style. There is never a period when it is safe to generalize without making numerous exceptions, but it does seem that, from 1520 to the end of the century, the nude was freely recognized as an important, perhaps the most important subject, for painting, for sculpture, and for drawing — which during this period became an independent branch of art as well as serving other purposes in the planning of paintings. The artist whom many regard as the foremost of all painters of the nude, Titian, is certainly not a Mannerist, and Correggio anticipates a style — the Baroque — that came into favour long after his death. With these exceptions, all the great nudes of the 16th century are the work of Mannerists: Michelangelo, Perino del Vaga, Parmigianino, Salviati, Rosso, Primaticcio, Niccolo dell' Abbate. Whatever other subjects they depicted, they were famous above all for depictions of the nude — and usually of the female nude.

Beccafumi and Pontormo, almost alone among the great Mannerists, seem to have spent little time on the nude, but whether this was from personal choice or because they were so busy with church commissions it is not easy to say. Even Leonardo, who is perhaps best studied in his drawings because so many of his projects

Hendrick Goltzius (1558–1617), Nymph and Satyr, late John Brophy Collection.

4

came to nothing, at least once entered into open competition with his fellow Florentine, Michelangelo. In 1504 they each submitted a cartoon: a large drawing setting out with some precision a project for a picture with the figures realized in detail. Both cartoons have long since disappeared and are known only through fragments, sketches, and copies, but each was full of nude figures, and each was for some years exhibited at the Palazzo Vecchio. Not only Florentines but artists from other parts of Italy and from other countries analyzed them, copied them, and learned from them, and it is perhaps from this two-man, two-piece exhibition, more than from any other single source, that the great tradition of Florentine Mannerism, and especially of the use of the nude body as a constructional element in large decorations, arises. Michelangelo and Leonardo may also have competed in treating the subject of 'Leda and the Swan'. Again their versions have disappeared, and we have only copies. Michelangelo's version, said to derive from an antique engraving for a gem, survives in a few old copies, of which the best known perhaps is that at the

National Gallery, London. Two variants of Leonardo's composition were copied in paint, but we have also copies of his drawings (fig. 2). The subject is highly erotic but completely misunderstood by Renaissance and later artists, for a swan becomes a phallic symbol only in flight, when its neck is outstretched.

From Florence, Mannerism was to spread back to Rome (with the brothers Zuccaro) where, in a sense, it had begun in the Sistine Chapel; north to Parma (where the majestic frescoes, 'Maidens' of Parmigianino in the Steccata Church are still too little known); northeast to Venice and across the Alps to France, where its influence can still be traced in some of the work of Picasso and Matisse. It spread also northeast into what is now Austria, Czechoslovakia, and Germany, for the pictorial arts, like music and — despite differences of language — literature, often set up a two-way traffic across frontiers. In the 15th and 16th centuries Italian artists went to other countries by invitation, and the invitation usually came from a monarch with a new palace to decorate. The prestige of Italian art was enormous and unquestionable, and it worked also in reverse: painters from northern countries came to Italy — especially to Venice, Florence, and Rome — and each stayed a number of years to study the "monuments", the surviving buildings, and sculptures of the Ancient World, to study the work of their Italian contemporaries; and to have their own work studied. Painters have never scorned to steal from each other, and progress in the pictorial arts is largely a matter of imitation, inflection, and adaptation. Cranach, who never visited Italy, became Mannerist in his old age and developed a highly popular, Italianate-German female nude (Plates 27-28). Dürer, who go not farther into Italy than Venice, learned from Italian examples (notably that of Leonardo) that an artist could live like a gentleman. Others after him, including Hans von Aachen and Bartolomeus Spranger, Netherlanders and Mannerists in the Italian style, achieved high social standing as Court painters at Munich and Prague.

The French did not travel so readily until the 18th century, and then they made for Rome where, safely housed in a French-speaking Academy, they did not need to feel that they had utterly cut themselves off from civilization — which so many Frenchmen used to equate with France, much as Louis XIV equated the State with himself. At the end of the 16th century, England — supreme in literature but lagging in the pictorial arts — sent Inigo Jones, who fell in love with Parmigianino's drawings as well as with the elegant architecture of Palladio. Many of the Germans and Netherlanders settled for as long as a decade in Florence. In the entourage of Vasari when he was decorating the Palazzo Vecchio, which still dominates the civic centre of Florence, were Frederich Sustris, Italian born but the son of Lambert Sustris of Amsterdam, and Peter Candid from Bruges, who both went on to work in Munich; and Jan van der Straet (Stradanus), also from Bruges, who died in Florence at the age of 82. The Lorrainer, Jacques Callot, was working there a little later, and while later Florentine Mannerism — led by Poccetti, Furini, Cigoli (fig. 3), and others — is largely devotional, the decorative Mannerism, which relies so much on nude figures, was made known all over Europe by Northerners — such as Bloemart, Marten de Vos, Cornelis Cornelisz of Haarlem, Goltzius (fig. 4), Jacques de Gheyn (fig. 5), and Uytewael — whose style was highly Italianate although some of them never set foot in Italy.

Francis I, having failed to get Leonardo, invited the Florentine he thought next in importance, Rosso, to design decorations for Fontainebleau, an elegant palace in the woods outside Paris. This was an odd choice to be made by a monarch as candidly erotic in his tastes as the Emperor Rudolf II, the patron of Spranger and Hans von Aachen, for Rosso was a neurotic and almost a religious visionary. The monarch, however, took the precaution of employing also Primaticcio, a Bolognese, who had worked under Giulio Romano at Mantua where he contributed some stylized stucco reliefs to the otherwise coarsely conceived decorations. Rosso died in 1540 (according to Vasari, by suicide out of mortification because he had brought a false charge against another artist), and almost certainly it is Primaticcio who should be regarded as the true founder of the School of Fontainebleau. His principal assistant, who seems to have surrendered his own quite charming style to Primaticcio's domination, was another Bolognese, Niccolo dell' Abbate. The Fontainebleau style — because it was elegant, erotic, and aristocratic — made (partly through engravings) one aspect of Mannerism immensely popular in the 16th century and ever since. French art was under the influence of Italy almost from the start and to an extent that is rarely acknowledged. Benvenuto Cellini spent some time in Paris and left behind him a bronze relief, 'The Nymph of Fontainebleau' (now at the Louvre) from which, and from the three-dimensional stone carving, the 'Diane' at the Chateau d'Anet (now also at the Louvre), generations of French artists drew inspiration. The 'Diane' may have been sculptured by Jean Goujon, and the delicate, proud face is doubtless the face of Diane, Duchess of Poitiers, but the whole figure of the goddess with the stag closely follows a drawing by Salviati, whose 18 months in France go almost unnoticed by art historians. The claim of Paris to be the leader and arbiter of fashions in dress, especially in women's dress, and in all the less-serious pictorial arts is often dated from early 17th century. But the prevailing taste of the Court of Louis XIV was more pompous than elegant, and a truer account might start with Fontainebleau rather than Versailles. During most of the hundred years after 1520, the dominant art of Italy was Mannerist, except in Venice where Tintoretto, Schiavone, and Palma Giovane were rare exceptions to the rule that Venetians need to be either Classical-Renaissance or Mannerist in style. Painters like Titian, Veronese, and the Bassanos solved the problem by being simply Venetian. Mannerism was even more dominant in France, and in Germany, Austria, and Switzerland it branched into the bizarre in the drawings, engravings, and occasional paintings of Grünewald, Nikolas Manuel Deutsch, Holbein, and Urs Graf who specialized in young naked witches flying — or about to fly — on their symbolic broom sticks. Spain imported from Crete, by way of Venice, a powerfully eccentric Mannerist ready made — El Greco. In the Netherlands, although ideas different from Mannerism but different also from those of the High Renaissance were about to come into favour, the Italianates commanded the field in the early years of the 17th century.

The hundred years from, roughly, 1520 might well be called the first great age of the nude in art since the breakup of the Roman Empire. It was an age, however, in which nakedness was depicted without any excessive determination to make the picture closely resemble real life. Nor was the nude often a self-sufficient subject. It was incidental to story-telling pictures, the stories drawn from a slowly expanding repertory of Greek and Roman myths, legends, and historical episodes, much as a repertory of religious subjects from the Old Testament, the New Testament, the Lives of the Saints, and Church history had been accumulated over the centuries by painters meeting the demands of churchmen patrons. The patrons of Mannerist painters, not all of them laymen, sometimes wanted devotional pictures, but it was probably they who created the demand for a new repertory of subjects taken from the Bible or other religious sources, which nevertheless allowed the portrayal of the nude, and especially the female nude. Among the most popular of these were David and Bathsheba (which supplied a Peeping Tom element psychologists would call 'voyeurism'), Susannah and the Elders (in some pictures the Elders look disconcertingly young to 20th-century eyes), and the seduction of the drunken Lot by his daughters.

The distinctive quality of later, sophisticated Mannerist nudes is elongation. From Botticelli onwards, arms and legs are made exceptionally slender, and long, thin fingers (sometimes tapering fingers) emerge gracefully from narrow hands and fine-boned wrists. In Parmigianino, and especially in Primaticcio and later Fontainebleau artists, the head may be noticeably small in proportion to the shoulders; the trunk is likely to be either a narrow column, or, if it is broad at the top, it will incline inwards sharply from the armpits to the waist, in a way reminiscent of some of the brown or black figures painted on old Greek vases. In Primaticcio's frescoes, and also in some Parmigianino, Salviati, and Niccolo dell' Abbate drawings, a most charming refinement is observable in the shaping of women's legs: the outline from haunch to knee traces a delicate inswing that merges into a longer outswing before the leg narrows quite sharply above the knee. This also perhaps has a Greek origin. Among Greek terracottas, often as a whole named Tanagra after the place in Boeotia where a large 'find' was made in 1870, Mannerist female figures occur quite often. This is especially so in late (2nd-1st century B.C.) figures from Myrina. It is probable that Mannerist elongations are not 'period' but timeless. All the Mannerist conventions can be paralleled in real life, but women so shaped are comparatively rare. They are not what manufacturers of women's dresses — who presumably have statistics to back their opinions —

would call 'average'. It is worth noting, however, that since the 1920s the mannequins employed by the leading 'fashion designers' of the world have, most of them, been exceptionally slender in body and limb, and it looks as though the Mannerist idea of feminine beauty was one to which many women, as well as men, subscribe.

It is less easy to define a Mannerist convention for depicting the face, and of many Mannerists it can be said that they seem to have been far more interested in the body, at least when they were depicting nudes. Tintoretto's male faces and Parmigianino's faces of men and women and children — despite the metallic glint he sometimes imparts to hair and beards — are the most sensitive, the most indicative of thought and feeling. Bronzino's faces, like his bodies, are apt to look as though they were made of highly glazed pale porcelain. Mannerism is often expounded as a neurotic product of the unruly and uncertain times in which it was created though it is doubtful they were any worse than the preceding decades, when Raphael and others were painting serenely in the Classical style, or any worse than the succeeding decades, full of savage religious controversy and bloody wars, during which Mannerism was counter-attacked, and most successfully, from at least three directions. Against the contention that Mannerism was essentially a neurotic phenomenon there can be argued the anomalous fact that, while they rebelled against the sedate, symmetric treatment of the human body by the High Renaissance, Mannerist painters in one important detail ignored the example of Michelangelo: they were content to render the faces that crowned their elegantly shaped, elegantly posed female bodies according to the serene, symmetric Classical ideal.

chapter 7

A number of artistic styles that developed as separate reactions against the prevalence of Mannerism can be detected in works done before 1600. But their flourishing period, when they were in full favour (sometimes all of them simultaneously) and when they displaced Mannerism in different parts of Europe, was the first half of the 17th century. In Italy there was a doctrinal reversion towards the Classical ideal. Associated with the three Carracci and the Academy (which they founded as early as 1586) at Bologna, this was a movement that did not always practice what it preached, for some of the paintings, done by Annibale and Agostino Carracci, are Mannerist enough to show the influence of Parmigianino. In basing its principles on drawing, from antique sculpture and from the life, the Carracci style did not greatly differ from what was being taught at the Academy at Florence (founded in 1563 while Michelangelo was still alive), but it is open to a charge of eclecticism because it picked out methods and effects from High Renaissance artists it approved of and sought to bind them into a generalized classical style. The greatest achievements of the Bolognese Carracci is in Rome, in the Gallery of the Palazzo Farnese, where vividly coloured frescoes, interspersed with monochrome paintings simulating stucco sculptures, celebrate a kind of New Look at the Ancient World. It was near the end of his life that Annibale Carracci imagined and, with assistance, realized in paint all these handsome young gods disporting with goddesses, nymphs, and naiads over ceilings and walls, in a lively though dignified pageant of nakedness. From the Carracci Academy came a whole line of Bolognese artists, including Guido Reni, Domenichino, Guericino, and Canuti, who were greatly admired into the 18th century but afterwards became a by-word for false sentiment and pretentiousness. Recently they have been taken seriously by a small band of art historians whose attempt to retrieve their reputations is regarded by other art historians as misguided and extravagant.

The Carracci have little to do with another Roman art movement, except in so far as it was an attempt to find an alternative opposing pole to Mannerism. The alternative was found in a minutely exact rendering of appearances. Strangely enough, the two younger Carracci, Annibale and Agostino, had a gift for depicting such realistic subjects as street scenes or a butcher's shop, so that the artists, had they been born in the Netherlands half a century later or in England about 1850, might have outdone Teniers, Ostade, or W. P. Frith. The Roman naturalism, however, of the early 17th century, in which Caravaggio was preeminent, is of a different kind. It is lush and makes much of the textures of fruits and silks and velvets and of the play of light over them. It imports a low-life atmosphere into religious pictures and abstracted not only the idealism from mythological subjects but also most of the grace and charm. Its nudes are believable but hardly interesting. Emotionally it is low toned. It appealed to the appetites rather than the senses, and its total implication seems to be that life is just one damn thing after another — neither spiritual, intellectual, nor fanciful.

Caravaggio's importance in the history of art has been magnified lately, in terms that are often disputable, but there can be little doubt that his gift for creating an illusion of artificial lighting, especially of candlelight, within the picture frame — he does not seem to have attempted fresco — set up a new *genre*. Painters such as Ribera, Honthorst, Terbruggen, Georges de la Tour, and the Le Nains owe much to him. More important is the influence of his work on one of the most prolific and popular of all the great painters — Rembrandt. From the turn of the century, the Netherlands, declaring their independence of Spain and growing swiftly into a maritime trading power, produced a larger number of artists who, as the 17th century progressed, more or less invented new kinds of pictures for a new kind of picture buyer.

The painters, etchers, and engravers of the Netherlands kept alive the Renaissance classical tradition in religious and other story-telling pictures — Rembrandt himself was trained under Pieter Lastman, whose style was quite Italian — and continued an Italianate Mannerism. They also became internationally famous for 'cabinet pictures'. These were small oil paintings, often done on wood panels, which, even when put into broad frames, could be displayed, six, eight, twelve at a time, on the walls of a single, not-very-large room. 'Cabinet pictures' and larger paintings, too, were bought in great numbers by the middle class, professional men as well as merchants. Among the new types of pictures popularized in this way were landscapes — until the 17th century, landscape was rarely, if ever, a subject in itself — flower pieces and still lifes of musical instruments, wine and wine glasses, gold and silver dishes, fruits, fish, meat, butter, cheese, and bread. It is said that such still lifes were in great demand because Dutch trading successes had produced a *nouveau riche* society whose members wanted to show that they could afford expensive things and even afford to have them pictured with the utmost verisimilitude. However much, or little, truth there is in this explanation, a great deal of Dutch 17th-century art aimed at reporting facts without suppression, without distortion, without ostensible sentiment. Instead of idealized figures from myth, legend, or history, arranged to suit the preconceptions of either Classical or Mannerist theory, Dutch realists portrayed their own contemporaries going about their daily routines. They wanted their pictures, large or small, and whatever the subject, to be believable.

When Rembrandt put Samson, Aristotle, Jason, and Moses into pictures, he made them look like Dutchmen and painted them as if neither the Ancient World nor Renaissance Italy had ever existed. When he took a classical myth as his subject, to paint a female nude, he produced a Danaë of a kind never seen before in art; we should know she was Dutch even if we did not know that he used his wife, Saskia, as his model. Similarly, when he undertook another of the recognized nude subjects, Bathsheba (Plate 60), he produced a picture of a naked woman which, as a complete composition and in detail, inch by inch over the whole surface of the canvas, is clearly a product of the Netherlands and the first half of the

17th century, and just as clearly is the work of Rembrandt in particular. The fact that Rembrandt's work, drawings and engravings as well as pictures, has proved and sustained its appeal in all countries, including Italy, and to all sorts of people for more than three centuries continuously may perhaps obscure his originality. What in effect he said was: "It is not necessary to follow either the Italian Renaissance line or the Gothic line to make beautiful pictures — and I will show you how!"

Technically a good deal of the new conception of beauty that Rembrandt introduced can be credited to his virtuoso skill in applying oil paints to canvas or wood — but there is more to it than that. He was a realist with a difference, and the difference was that he presented his realism in a romantic light. Often, though not always, it was lamplight or candlelight, set off by gradations of shadow and with tints of gold dominant. It is interesting that a debt to Caravaggio can be traced, but perhaps the most impressive thing about Rembrandt is that his own influence was so long lived. His work looks forward to the 19th century, to the emotional stimulation discovered in colour by Géricault, Delacroix, and other Romantics and to the use of light by the Impressionists as not an adjunct to a picture but its *raison d'être.*

Rembrandt's drawings are also realistic and, one might say, almost anti-Italian. Neither of his (unpaid) models, Saskia and Hendrickje Stoffels, would have had much chance of sitting for an Italian artist; their bodies were the wrong shape, and their faces would have been considered plain. Rembrandt saw them as beautiful, and made them beautiful, not only in paint but in numerous drawings, many done with a broad reed pen sliding and scribbling across the paper and making hardly one clean curve among all the angular jabs and cross-hatching and blotches. What emanates from the uninked parts of the paper is a shimmering luminosity, as white as the light in the paintings is golden, and just as romantic. It is an effect Rembrandt could not have calculated in advance, and no one, in retrospect, can either explain it or explain it away. The evocative or magical use of white space in drawings, although always rare, is more often found when monochrome washes, applied with a brush, reinforce the pen strokes. Strangely, Rembrandt is not often at his best with wash, of which the masters include Cambiaso, G. B. Tiepolo, and Rodin.

The contrasts between Rembrandt and Rubens (whose lifetimes overlap by 34 years) are so sharp that they can hardly be diminished by familiarity. Rembrandt stayed at home, was middle class in outlook, ignored Italian influence, and went bankrupt. Rubens was rich, was a successful diplomat as well as a successful painter, mingled with kings and cardinals, fell under the spell of Italy in his youth, and often conducted his correspondence in Italian. Rembrandt painted very few nudes, though two of them are superb. Rubens is one of the most prolific of all celebrants of naked female beauty. Despite his awareness of the Italian

5

Jacques de Gheyn (1565–1629), Prometheus, late John Brophy Collection.

tradition, he was as Flemish as Rembrandt was Dutch; he founded a new Flemish school of painting, which overspilled into England (where he was knighted); and he taught the whole world to admire, as beautiful, a type of woman with what might seem considerable physical handicaps.

The Rubens beauty — and he painted hundreds of them — is large and formidable, more vigorous than either Titian's golden-brown ladies drowsing in Venetian sunshine or Michelangelo's symbolic Florentines carved in tawny marble. Rubens' women are quite capable of propelling a symbolic galleon with symbolic oars or, impersonating the Three Graces, holding a huge basket of flowers high above their heads, the better to show off their substantial bosoms and haunches. Even when they are being carried away by amorous young men, the women of Rubens, although they are obviously capable of violent resistance if they wished, appear to enjoy the situation more than their captors –– who have been prudent enough to bring powerful horses for the removal of their weighty prizes. Rubens women almost always have gold or light brown hair, and their skin, distended by intense pressure from within (but not marred by that resemblance to a mass of balloons which many Giulio Romano women have) is fair, Northern, translucent, compounded of whites and creams with incidental touches of pale green and blue and pink.

Rubens, one feels, could paint anything he wished, from trees to insects, and his drawing is as skilful as any, but possibly the greatest of all his technical achievements is his vivid rendering of the large lush nakedness of Flemish women. Often his models were his wives: first the fine-boned, slightly hollow-cheeked Isabella Brandt; later Hélène Fourment, with the large, round, swimming, and protuberant eyes which she transmitted to her children. He painted his wives as Venus, as Juno, as Diana, as anonymous nymphs, and as quite bare allegorical females crowning heroes with laurel wreaths or ornamenting the various episodes of the life of Marie de Medici. Whether he painted with the model-spouse posed in front of his easel, or from a stock of drawings and oil sketches previously accumulated, we cannot always be sure. Indeed, we cannot always be sure which of the two successive wives was the inspiration for a particular picture, for in some portraits of Isabella Brandt there is more than a hint of the pop-eyed look that Hélène Fourment shared with her sister Susanne, whom he also painted often. Rubens himself, according to the evidence of several portraits, was rather spare of flesh and fine of feature, with eyes that could be described as normal: neither small nor large and certainly not protuberant. It looks as though, as with many of us, he responded to the sexual attraction of bodily characteristics in the other sex that were the opposite of his own. If so, it is one more instance of the human tendency to seek out situations of polarity.

chapter 8

The most spectacular style of the 17th century was the Baroque — in German *Barock* — and its nature is such that it has ever since attracted more attention than, in the view of many people, its merits deserve. It can fairly be called the dominant style, so far as architecture and large public decorations go, from about 1630 to the end of the century, in Rome and France, and later in southern Germany and Austria. In Holland, Northern Germany, and the Scandinavian countries, Baroque art is scarce. It is practically unknown in Great Britain. The word does not seem to have been admitted to the English language before 1851, and the Oxford Dictionary, before summarizing its meaning as "irregularly shaped; grotesque; odd", derives it from a Portuguese name for a "rough pearl". It would not be unfair to say that most people in Northern Europe, and most Americans, Canadians, and Australians of North European origin, find the Baroque style distasteful, although they may have learned to make distinctions between "good of its kind" and "terrible". It is difficult to be objective about the Baroque if only because its aim seems to be to overwhelm and confuse the senses, and thereby to play on the emotions. Instinctively many people resent this. The application of the word *Baroque* to particular paintings and sculpture is often debatable. Rubens, Rembrandt, Poussin, and Caravaggio — though often claimed as Baroque artists, at least in certain works — hardly fulfill any but a generalized definition. To call them Baroque is perhaps saying no more than that they lived and worked in the 17th century. At certain places during that century, a flamboyant taste required, and admired, emotionality in religious art. Versailles was setting a new and lavish fashion in palaces. Maderna, Borromini, and other architects working for the Jesuits in Rome were establishing a new theatrical look for churches.

So far from being a simple reaction against Mannerism, the Baroque style in painting seems to be attempting some of the same ends and by not-altogether-different methods. It is representational and uses human bodies, vigorously in action, as components of elaborate designs. It aims at creating intricate illusions of three dimensions within the limits of two. When it makes fake sculptures in paint it is merely following an example set by Rosso, Primaticcio and Veronese. The differences, however, are striking. Mannerist art is, by comparison, intellectual. It may try to allure the spectator with suggestions of sexuality; it hardly ever, if at all, invites him to an orgy of religious exhilaration. In the treatment of pagan themes the Baroque is a style on its own: Pietro da Cortona, for example, is as gay in colour in his Barberini Palace ceilings as Annibale Carracci at the Palazzo Farnese only a mile or two away in Rome, but in content and general effect these and other Baroque paintings tend to be earnestly allegorical. What is required of the spectator — the general public — is submission to the religious pictures, assent to the allegories.

The required effect is obtained by illusion, by pushing the logic of Renaissance experiments with perspective still further, so that instead of looking up at a big ceiling we have the sensation of looking up at real sky and real clouds, framed within architecture that blends illusionistic paint into actual stone and plaster. The sky is thronged with angels, saints, prophets, and patriarchs, or — if the subject should be allegorical — by an alternative cast of gods, goddesses, heroes, and nymphs. Sacred or profane, the skyborne figures trail and flutter coloured robes so ingeniously that they seem to palpitate and undulate while they soar among the clouds. The effect is exhilarating or depressing, solemn or unintentionally absurd, according perhaps to one's temperament, taste, or even mood. What everyone may agree on is that some very gifted artists spent their gifts gladly enough in the belief that the Baroque was both novel and sublime.

The Baroque was little concerned with the nude, and its interest in the face was almost all concentrated on portraiture. This is not surprising if the proposition is accepted that essentially the Baroque is an architectural style and not only subordinates painting to architecture (this was a notion held by many a Renaissance painter) but subordinates the human figure, in scale and in importance, to its grandiose domes and porticos. Bernini, the Roman sculptor, architect, and painter, is generally considered to be the originator of the Baroque, and there is no reason to dispute the judgment. What is interesting, however, is that Bernini is not exactly the sort of artist we should expect to be the founding father of such a style. His sculptures and his drawings, if we did not know otherwise, might well look late Florentine — that is to say Mannerist. The great colonnade which he invented and erected in two enveloping curves from the front of St Peter's has few, if any, Baroque characteristics. It is, predominantly, High Renaissance in feeling. His marble 'Ecstasy of St Theresa' — although undeniably Baroque in the intense religious emotion it communicates — seems to present, and with similar emphasis, the sort of subject which, a century before, Rosso had painted and Bandinelli had modelled in relief. When we remember that Bernini was a brilliant caricaturist

— his head-and-shoulders sketch of Cardinal Scipio Borghese might have been drawn in the 20th century to make a 'line block' — we must concede to his art an altogether exceptional range. What is most startling, perhaps, is the chapel at the little church of Santa Maria della Vittoria in Rome where the St Theresa sculpture is housed. Designed by Bernini himself, the chapel is full of innovating colour and light and variety of texture, and if we did not know it was by Bernini, the founder of the solemn Baroque, we might easily and happily consider it Rococo.

When Giovanni Battista Tiepolo was born in 1696, the Baroque style had almost run its course in Italy. Far away on the northern side of the Alps, Antoine Watteau was then a 12-year-old boy in Valenciennes, a Flemish town recently incorporated into France. With Watteau — whose art is paradoxally *triste,* even tragic — began the gay, ingenious decades of frivolity with a style now known as Rococo. Tiepolo outlived Watteau by almost 50 years — yet Tiepolo is generally accounted the last, the belated, master of the Baroque and its greatest decorator, perhaps the greatest decorator the world has ever known. It was presumably because of the Baroque qualities that his work fell out of favour during the 19th century. He has other qualities — a sprightliness in his figures, even the figures of aged men symbolizing time, and a fondness for lemon yellows and lime greens laid alongside cream and white — that may be accounted positively Rococo. His greatest works are outside Venice, at Madrid and Würzburg. (Plates 61–62), but perhaps in assessing his achievement both the not-so-solemn Baroque and the transcended Rococo elements in his work are less important than his Venetian inheritance from Titian, Tintoretto, and Veronese. Among the advantages which Venice, like England, derived from being a great maritime trading power was the importation of foreign talents. Andrea Schiavone, who introduced an infusion of Parmigianino's idyllic grace into Venetian art, was — as his name suggests — a Slav. He arrived from Dalmatia and started almost literally at the bottom of the ladder — as a house-painter. El Greco, whose art was strongly influenced by Tintoretto and the Bassanos, came from Crete which then belonged to Venice, and his family name, Theotocopoulos, is thought by some to be the full Greek version of a name which, after several generations, became Italianised as Tiepolo.

Rococo is at the opposite pole from Baroque. It seems to belong to France and Northern Germany rather than to Rome, Munich, and Vienna, although it is to be seen in all three cities. Rococo is Boucher and Fragonard (Plates 67–68). It is garlands of pink and yellow roses upheld by plump cupids too knowing ever to pass themselves off as angels. It is goddesses

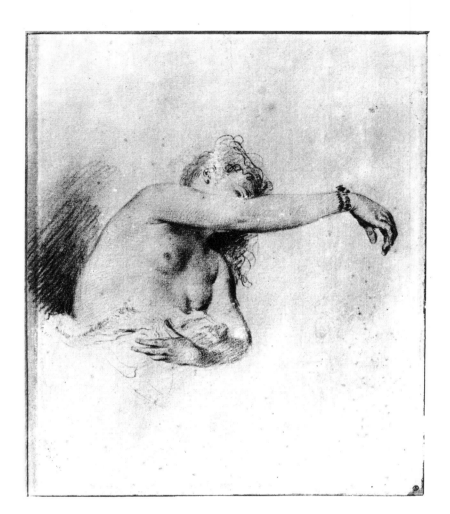

6

making slow but stately progress through idyllic woodland glades with never a lock disturbed in the elaborately arranged hair that rises 12 inches or more above their serene faces adorned with dainty beauty patches. Rococo is little teenage girls dabbling their feet and hands in summertime brooks, and passing the winter indoors by reclining on satin cushions, with an elegantly framed mirror not far away on wall or ceiling. Foremost among the pink and white Rococo girls is Mlle. Marie Louise O'Morphi, born in Paris, the child of parents forced to emigrate from Dublin, and mistress of Louis XV. François Boucher drew and painted her, for the dreary monarch's delectation, with considerable skill but was unable to invest her snub-nosed, pouting little face with as much personality as her frequently upturned bottom. Rococo is fanciful and frivolous curves — they can be seen in Dresden china tea services and in the façades of buildings in Amsterdam and The Hague as well as in the spreading skirts, the looped-up *tricorne* hats, the chandeliers, the lanterns, the tables and chairs, and the lightly sprung carriages of the period. Rococo is not easy to find in churches — it is a boudoir art if ever there was one —

except in Bavaria and Austria, where there survive quite a large number with interiors apparently made of white icing sugar, their ceilings brilliantly painted by Maupertsch or Ignaz Günther.

Rococo is almost at its best in France and with Fragonard (Plates 67–68) whose mastery of drawing may have been inferior to Boucher's but who retained a kind of Provençal, almost bucolic naturalness even when he was executing aphrodisiac commissions for Madame du Barry or others of his rich patrons. The Rococo often went in danger of becoming absurd, not because, like the Baroque, it easily became pompous, but because intemperance was part of its nature. It was the style of an Age of Reason, or Age of Unbelief, and perhaps it did not even believe in itself very strongly.

Its greatest artist was its earliest, Watteau, and he perhaps marks the frontier where Rococo is separated from Baroque. It is a strange and tenuous link, for at first sight no two artists could seem further apart than Rubens and Watteau. Rubens was the painter of huge canvases and ceilings and of women big of bosom and thigh; extrovert in temperament, aristocratic in a hearty, well-fed, bourgeois way; and almost all of them apparently ready to join the dance at a Flemish Kermesse even if, for the sake of the Baroque conventions, it is being passed off as a strictly allegorical occasion. With Watteau the scale is entirely different. His largest pictures are still small ones, and it would be hard, if not impossible, to find any depiction by him of a human being life size. Watteau's women are exquisitely painted, or exquisitely drawn in red and white chalks (fig. 6). Their bodies are neat and compact, delicately shaped and slender. They are out for enjoyment, in true Rococo fashion, and their life appears to be a perpetual *fête galante,* but their senses are refined to rare and poignant perceptions. Like the lovers who accompany them, they are dreamers, and their dreams may be amorous or even sensual, but not gross. They would draw back in disgust, one feels, from the mere sound at a distance of a Rubens Kermesse. Yet Watteau is not only as Flemish (or Northern French) as Rubens but was a close student, and often an imitator, of Rubens' work. To him Rubens must have appeared to be a master who, though long dead, came from the same countryside and spoke to him in his own language. There are many examples of this hidden and belated master-and-disciple relationship. One of the most striking is Watteau's little painting at the Louvre, 'The Judgment of Paris', which shows Venus pulling her robe over her head to stand naked before the shepherd. It is one of the few 18th-century works which for charm and delicacy can compare with Giorgione's 'Sleeping Venus' at Dresden or Raphael's 'Three Graces' at Chantilly. The Venus is taken, however, with only minor modifications, from a large Rubens drawing, now in the Louvre Print Room.

chapter 9

Rococo came to an end with the French Revolution. Boucher was already dead. Fragonard lost his patrons and his popularity and lived on, almost forgotten, till the year of Trafalgar. The ending was not sudden. Some years before the events of 1789 public taste was being led by a couple of earnest Germans living in Rome — Winckelmann and the painter, Mengs — towards a new set of artistic principles. Neo-classicism drew its authority from studies of the ruins and remains excavated at Pompeii and Herculaneum, and in particular from low-relief sculptures. These newly uncovered antiquities were made known to the world through careful pen drawings reproduced as engravings. A technique of delineating forms by outlines unvarying in breadth was taken up by Flaxman in England, David in France, Thorwaldsen (a Dane

who lived for 40 years in Rome), Canova in Italy, and by many others. It became the fashion, and for a time, when David was all powerful in a revolutionary France just beginning a career of conquest, the Neo-classical doctrines had political force and standing.

Few people take an interest in Neo-classical paintings today except as documents of a phase in art history. Canova's sculpture is nearer to 20th-century taste (Plates 69–70). The paintings, by careful composition and posing of the figures, with the intention of maintaining an overall dignity, abstracted the undulating illusion of movement from the themes of both Baroque and Rococo art, disposed the robes into careful pleatings, and — emulating the effect of the old Roman low reliefs coming to light on the shores of the Bay of Naples — carried out the whole action of the pictures in a foreground apparently no more than a foot or two in depth.

Like a brittle eggshell, destined to be thrown aside, Neo-classicism contained within itself the potentials of two other art movements of the early 19th century. These were Romanticism, exemplified by Delacroix (Plates 75–76), and Realism, associated especially with Courbet (Plates 77–78). It was also, and ironically, involved with a revival of interest in Mannerism. For about 150 years, while first the Baroque and then Rococo flourished, the Mannerist art of the 16th century had been not so much despised as neglected. Now it began to interest a few artists. Johann Heinrich Füssli, the Swiss who became John Henry Fuseli and, though never a good painter, was a striking and original draughtsman, was appointed professor at the Royal Academy in London and exercised a deal of influence on leading painters including Lawrence and Romney. He had spent the years 1770 to 1778 in Rome, studying Michelangelo and other Mannerists. Fuseli's drawings are fantastic in a *Sturm und Drang* manner that may be ascribed to the period and to his German-Swiss origins. He imported a strong tincture of eroticism into postures and groupings which he adapted from Michelangelo. Some of his young women seem more naked than if they had been stripped bare; he drew them in long, pseudo-mediaeval gowns, with towering headdresses but with their breasts completely uncovered, like Cretan priestesses. It was probably through Fuseli that Blake, the poet, mystic, and illuminator — his work is all page size — learned to emulate, on a small scale, and in water colours, the grandeurs of the Sistine Chapel ceiling. Blake's drawings, however, have practically no erotic content. His visions are all high minded. He and Fuseli are belated Mannerists but of two different kinds.

More central to the future development of European art was the Mannerism to be seen in some of Géricault's work. One feels that he had in his own temperament a strongly disruptive dynamism, the same kind of force that provided the inner energy for Michelangelo and those of the 16th-century Mannerists who followed his lead and eschewed elegance and languours. It was perhaps in an attempt to control his own romantic obsession with violence that Géricault put himself, during his short lifetime, under two strict disciplines. He made numbers of sketches, of subjects from Greek myths and legends, using the Neo-classical technique, but he defeated his own object, with a unique effect, because of the violence of the poses and gestures he used and the nervous spontaneity of his delineatory lines and washed-in shadows. He was more controlled working from Mannerist designs (fig. 7) when, presumably, he found all the temperamental stimulus he needed in the original. A great deal of the Romantic theory which Delacroix — who lived till 1863 — theorized and put into practice may be traced back to Géricault's example, and 'The Death of Sardanapalus' (Plates 75–76) owes much to 'The Raft of the Medusa', as the proximity of the two huge paintings at the Louvre reveals.

The second discipline Géricault put on himself was sometimes to look quietly at everyday subjects — a smith shoeing a horse, a man ferrying a boat across a river — and make unstylized, literal transcripts of the visible facts onto paper. Like Bernini in the 17th century, Géricault is an artist at the crossroads, with a foot now in this direction, now in that. He is linked to Neo-classicism as a contemporary movement from which he could not afford to stand aside, and his Neo-classic phase links him, however improbable it sounds, to the High Renaissance by way of those worthy teachers who, in any of the modern periods, try to please the average man by serving up what they believe to be Raphaelesque subjects treated in a Raphaelesque manner. Géricault is linked also, by his own temperament and interest, to Mannerism as an antithesis of the Raphaelesque. He is linked, as a founder, to the Romantic movement of the early 1800s and, through his true-to-life drawings, to the later Realistic school headed by Courbet (Plates 77–78). The French Romantics, largely through the influence of the Anglophile Géricault, and perhaps through the emigré Bonnington, were stimulated to an interest in the experiments of the revolutionary English painter, Turner, who slapped brilliant colours onto canvas almost as haphazardly as any 20th-century Tachist. Turner himself, even more than Constable, played midwife unaware to the most powerful of all the art movements of the 19th century — Impressionism.

Those painters who became known as 'Impressionists' were not in full revolt against naturalism such as Courbet's. Their ambition was to depict the appearance of things more truthfully — by which they did not mean in greater detail. They professed, as their ideas clarified, to be studying, by experiment on canvas, the different ways light is affected by the various shapes and surface textures it touches. This led them towards an analytic investigation of tone and colour. The purest Impressionist practice was to paint grass and trees, sky and water, without preliminary sketches, direct onto canvas and in the open air. In this sense Monet, Sisley, and Pissarro have the best right to be called Impressionists. As it happens they are among the least important of the group and took little interest in the nude. The Impressionists were in fact of many kinds and differed widely in aims and methods. They made up an informally coherent association because, although some, like Manet, Degas, and Lautrec, had money and social position, they felt themselves to be excluded from an artistic 'establishment' centred on the Paris Salon and perpetuating a stale academic ideal only superficially brought up to date. Just as the opposite pole to the classical principles, as demonstrated in Raphael 'Madonna' pictures, might be either forceful Mannerism or elegant Mannerism or, some years later, Romanticism, so the competent but unexciting academic art of the 19th century produced several different kinds of painters in declared opposition.

Manet was one. He was influenced by Impressionist doctrines and examples, but basically he worked apart from the movement. Whatever he himself said, it is hard to believe that he cared much about scientific analyses of light and using the spectrum as an index to establish the right tone of the right colour for shadows. One feels that Manet was above all a practical painter who learned as much from the Old Masters, Velasquez certainly, Rubens almost certainly, and perhaps from Frans Hals with his technique of building what at close view are all too obviously brush marks into a total representational effect. Two of Manet's nudes made history. The 'Déjeuner sur l'herbe' (Plates 79–80) showed a naked young woman picnicking in a woodland glade with two young men who wore the full black and grey city clothing of 1863. This was a mixture which Titian and Giorgione had offered without protest — but they were acknowledged Old Masters and long-since dead. Manet's modernization of this subject was rejected by the Salon. Two years later his 'Olympia' passed the jury, but an immense scandal arose when it was put on exhibition.

The rumpus in the press and elsewhere gave impetus, and prestige as well, to the Impressionist movement, although neither of these Manet nudes abides by Impressionist principles. It was not until 1870, in fact, that Manet abandoned the use of black and began to paint shadows in colour; he was persuaded, it is said, to experiment with the new technique by his sister-in-law, Berthe Morisot, herself a charming and gifted painter, undervalued in her own time, and since — presumably because she was a woman. Renoir (Plates 83–84), nine years younger than Manet, as a boy painted designs onto unglazed porcelain in a china factory. This links him with the Rococo style, and it is not surprising to learn that he incessantly studied the works of Watteau, Boucher, and Fragonard at the Louvre. He is sometimes Impressionist, sometimes not, as in 'Les Parapluies' at the National Gallery.

Of the other three who complete the Impressionist hierarchy, Degas, Gauguin, and Toulouse-Lautrec, it can be said with some confidence that while they may be associated with the movement and its outlook, they do not belong to it. In Degas it is the drawing that matters. When he uses oil paints he is as ready as Botticelli to outline the forms with a clear, clean, continuous stroke of a brush used as if it were a pencil. Degas began representationally, with a style deriving from Corot and even from Ingres. He remained representational but found his own style, and his own subjects — washerwomen, ballet dancers, and any young woman without too much flesh on her bones, who would strip and pose with a bathtub at hand (Plates 81–82). Much of his work that is thought of, and spoken of, as painting is drawing in pastels — another name for chalks.

Gauguin (Plates 85–86) was in his thirties when he began to exhibit with the Impressionists. He discovered his best subjects and a style of his own only in the last years of his life. Like the Neo-classical paintings of a century earlier, his pictures provide a minimum illusion of depth, and his figures are hardly modelled at all. He was a pattern-making designer working with the greens and yellows and reds of semi-tropical vegetation but above all with the brown bodies and simplified, rather flat faces of the naked girls of Tahiti.

Toulouse-Lautrec (Plates 87–88), a draughtsman like Degas, is hardly a painter at all when compared with Manet and Renoir; when he did use oils he was apt to mix in a medium that left the pigment dried out on the surface with a pastel-like effect. In his own lifetime he was much praised but regarded as something of a journalist, one whose métier was to produce posters and other ephemeral illustrations of Parisian life. Of all the Impressionists Lautrec is the one who in his work shows the keenest and most penetrating interest in people as people. His life has become a popular legend with himself as an almost operatic figure, an aristocrat crippled in childhood, growing into a genius and a bohemian, and slowly killing himself with drink while he produced masterpiece after masterpiece. There is just enough truth in the legend to make it illuminating. Lautrec found his subjects in cafés, dance halls, and brothels. He tells the truth about his women, young and bony, old and bony, old and fat, young and exhausted, most of them with vicious and ugly faces, yet he romanticises the reality he records just as much as Rembrandt did. He romanticises partly because his drawing is itself beautiful, partly because his compositions are, through instinct or calculation, of a classical symmetry, but most of all because he is sympathetic towards singers and sluts, trulls, barmaids, and whores, and his tolerant understanding is always perceptible in his magical lines and his magical pattern-making of colour alongside colour.

chapter 10

Although we are now well advanced into the second half of the 20th century there is still no general agreement about which artists in the early decades of the century, or even which of the numerous artistic movements of that time, are the ones that matter. Some people consider that Post-Impressionism, founded on the works of Van Gogh (whose vision was as peculiar to himself as El Greco's) and Cézanne (a dogged painter with theories) will seem to posterity more important than Impressionism itself. Others champion Cubism or Expressionism or Surrealism. Our century has produced more conflicting, and confusing, philosophies, theories, and doctrines of art than all its predecessors put together, and agreement may never be reached because human beings do not see the same pictures with the same eyes and with the same pleasure or displeasure. Whichever school obtains a wide acceptance for its doctrines thereby incites others to be contrary, to find or invent an opposite doctrinal pole.

If opinion, taste, and valuation are always changing, they also change in relation to works of art done in the distant past and seemingly safe from pro-and-con arguments. We keep our minds alert by periodically shaking them up, and even our general views of history, our perspectives into the past, have no finality. We need not, therefore, be alarmed because we cannot reach a stable attitude towards Modigliani (Plates 93–94), for example, or Picasso (Plates 95–96), or Henry Moore (Plates 99–100). They are all too close to us. We shall be less tempted to impatience with our own limitations if we remember that some of the conceptions of the past which seem to us to have been part of "our common heritage" from "time immemorial" are in fact quite recent inventions. The Hellenes of the 5th century B.C. did not know that they were classical; nearly 2000 years had to pass before the

7

word in its usual modern sense was established. Many ideas we take for granted were new and startling not so long ago when they were put before our great grandparents. The idea of the Renaissance, for example, as the opening of a new age and as a series of historical events beginning in Italy during the 15th century was by no means clear to people living through those events, many of whom thought that what they were living through was all catastrophe and decline. The wide use of the word 'Renaissance' in the present sense is no older than the 18th century, and although we may wonder how historians and art critics got along without it, the sober fact is that the very word 'Renaissance' was unknown before 1840. 'Renaissance' is said, by Professor Hugh Trevor-Roper, to have been invented by the French historian Jean Michelet. This would account for the French form of the word, which has resisted all pedantic attempts to rewrite it as 'Renascence'. As 'Renaissance' the word, and the idea, were popularized all over Europe and America by another historian, the Swiss, Jakob Burckhardt, with his most influential book *The Civilization of the Renaissance in Italy,* first published in 1860. We must therefore assume that quite a long time will pass before the art of our own time is sorted out and evaluated, artist by artist, movement by movement, to the general satisfaction. We are too close to see clearly, and all our judgments on our contemporaries should be tentative. We must agree to disagree with each other, as courteously as our strong feelings will allow, about a great many pictures, drawings, and sculptures. There is one thing, however, most of us

can agree upon whether we like it or not — that there are in 20th-century art many tendencies, some of them powerful, that break away from the course set 500 years ago in Renaissance Italy and maintained, despite minor deviations, ever since. It is presumably because of such tendencies that, while some of the older living artists have demonstrated their skill in depicting the body and the face, these subjects do not hold the unquestioned primacy in art that they once did.

This may turn out to mean, when a truer historical perspective is reached, that we are now entering, in the second half of the 20th century, not a new period but a new age in the development of art, as different from its predecessor as the Renaissance was from the Middle Ages. If so, the Old Masters, and the Modern Masters of the 19th century and the early decades of the 20th, will take on an increased rarity value. Their nudes will seem to our children's children more beautiful than they are to us because by then a tradition will have come to an end for lack of artists trained, and skilful, enough to carry it on. If the supposition is wrong, however — if the subjects which were the chief subjects of art for the Greeks and the Romans and for all the great artists since the 15th century should come back into full favour — the credit for maintaining continuity should be given to a few painters but above all, some will think, to the sculptors, Bourdelle and Rodin, Mestrovic, Epstein, Maillol, Gaudier-Brzeska, Lehmbruck, and others who never stopped looking at the human body and finding it beautiful.

PLATES

Plates 1–2.   UNKNOWN EGYPTIAN ARTIST. '*Dancing Girls*'.

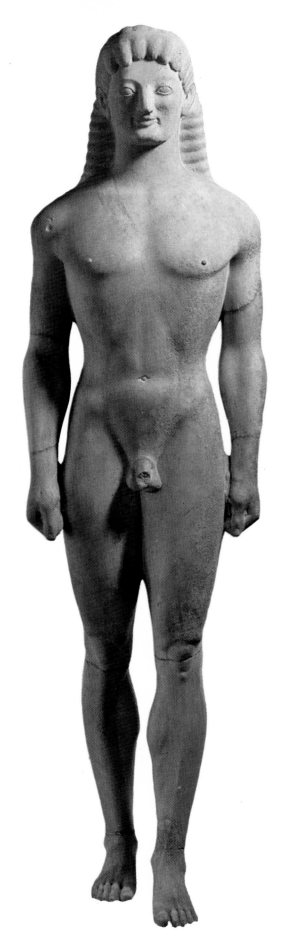

Plates 3–4.   UNKNOWN SCULPTOR. *'Apollo of Tenea'*.

Plates 5–6.   UNKNOWN HELLENISTIC SCULPTOR. 'The Medici Venus'.

Plates 7–8.   Unknown Artist in Pompeii. *'Perseus and Andromeda'*.

Plates 9–10. UNKNOWN ROMAN ARTIST. *'Girl Gymnasts'*.

Plates 11–12.   TILMAN RIEMENSCHNEIDER. *'Eve'*.

Plates 13–14.   LUCA SIGNORELLI. *'The Resurrection'.*

Plates 15–16.   GREGOR ERHART. '*Mary Magdalene*'.

Plates 17–18.   SANDRO BOTTICELLI. *'The Birth of Venus'*.

Plates 19–20.   LEONARDO DA VINCI. *'Half-length portrait of an Unknown Woman.'*

Plates 21–22.   ALBRECHT DÜRER. *'Eve'*.

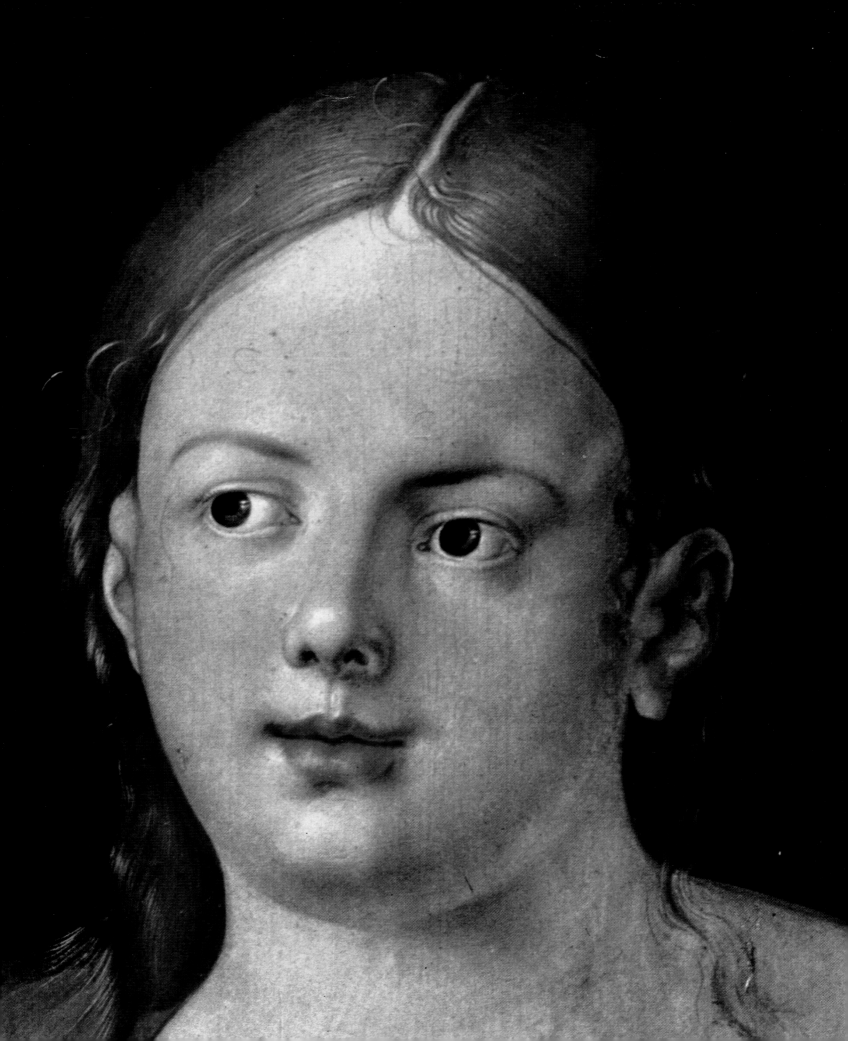

Plates 23–24.   MICHELANGELO. *'Dawn'*.

Plates 25–26.   RAPHAEL. *'The Triumph of Galatea'*.

Plates 27–28.   LUCAS CRANACH. *'Venus and Cupid With The Stolen Honey'*.

Plates 29–30. TITIAN. *'Danaë'.*

Plates 31–32.   CORREGGIO. *The Education of Cupid*.

Plates 33–34. BRONZINO, AGNOLO. *'Allegory'*.

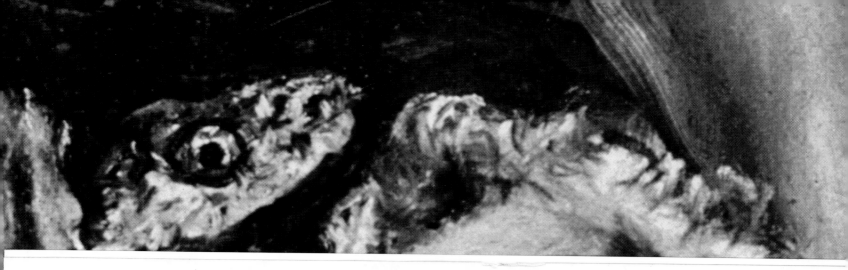

Plates 35–36.   Francesco Salviati. *'Charity'*.

Plates 39–40.   TINTORETTO. '*Susanna and the Elders*'.

Plates 41–42. EL GRECO. *'Laocoön'*.

Plates 43–44.   SCHOOL OF FONTAINEBLEAU. '*Diana Goddess of the Chase*'.

Plates 45–46.   PAOLO VERONESE. *'Venus and Mars'*.

Plates 47–48.   FRANÇOIS BUNEL. *A Lady at her Toilet'*.

Plates 49–50. CORNELIS CORNELISZ. *'The Wedding of Peleus and Thetis'*.

Plates 53–54.   JOOS VAN WINGHE. '*Apelles and Campaspe*'.

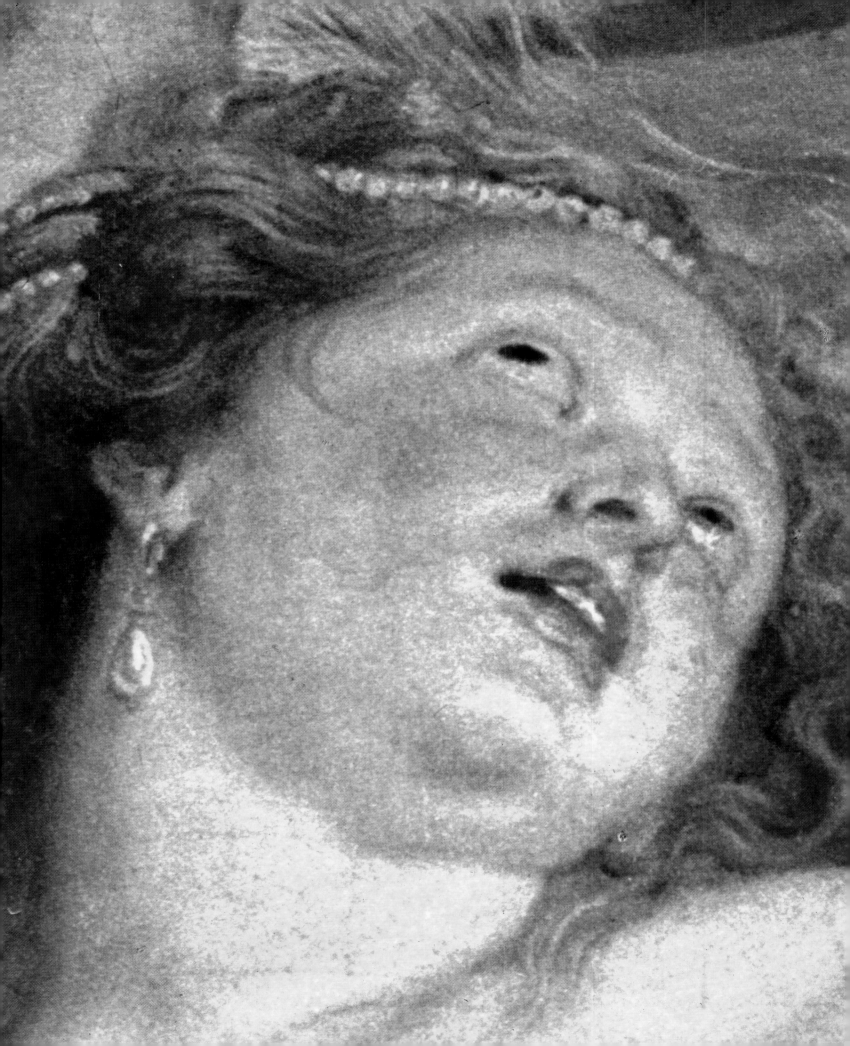

Plates 55–56.   PETER PAUL RUBENS. *'The Daughters of Leucippus Seized by Castor and Pollux'*.

Plates 57–58.   JACOB JORDAENS. *'Pan and Syrinx'*.

Plates 59–60.   REMBRANDT. *'Bathsheba'*.

Plates 61–62. GIOVANNI BATTISTA TIEPOLO. *'America'*.

Plates 63–64. FRANÇOIS BOUCHER. '*The Toilet of Venus*'.

Plates 65–66. THOMAS GAINSBOROUGH. *'Musidora'*.

Plates 67–68.   Jean-Honoré Fragonard. *'Girls Bathing.'* *('Les Baigneuses')*.

Plates 69–70.   Antonio Canova. *'Venus Victorious'*.

Plates 71–72.   JEAN BAPTISTE REGNAULT. *'The Three Graces'.*

Plates 73–74. JEAN AUGUSTE DOMINIQUE INGRES. *'The Spring'*.

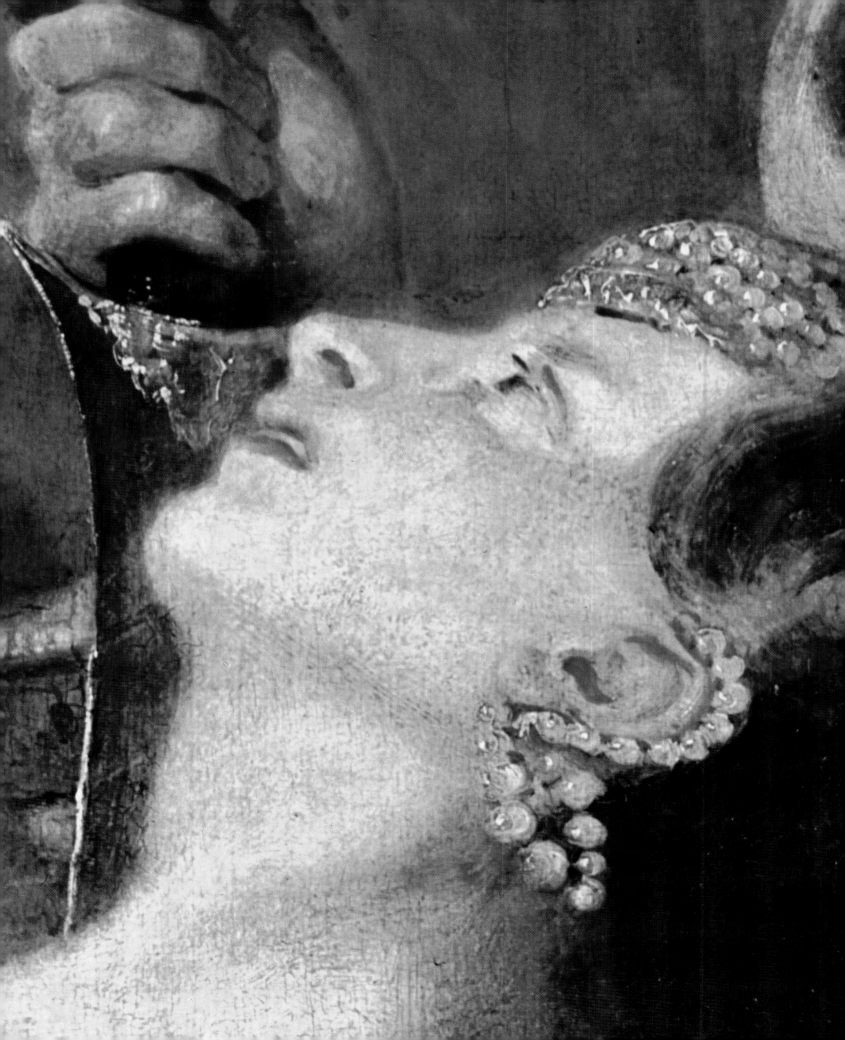

Plates 75–76.   EUGÈNE DELACROIX. *'The Death of Sardanapalus'*.

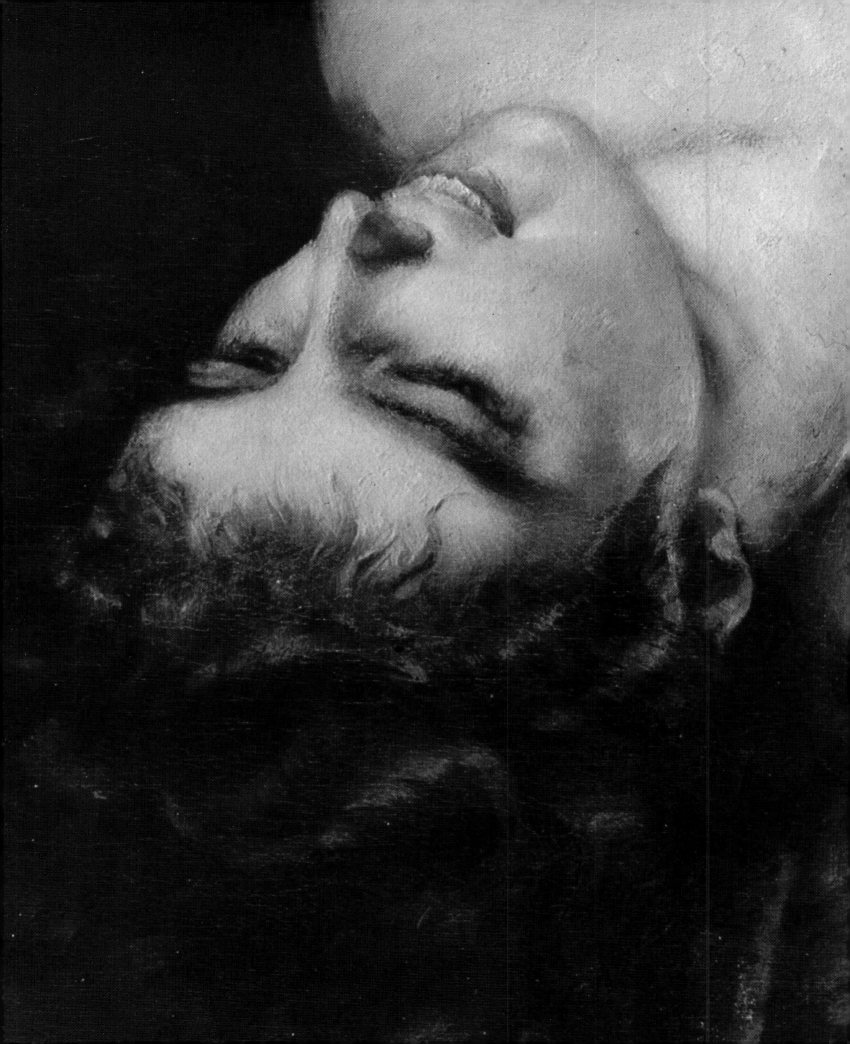

Plates 77–78.   GUSTAVE COURBET. *'The Woman With a Parrot'*.

Plates 79–80.   EDOUARD MANET. '*Déjeuner sur l'herbe*' ('*The Picnic*').

Plates 81–82.   EDGAR DEGAS. '*After the Bath*'

Plates 83–84.   PIERRE-AUGUSTE RENOIR. '*Nude on a Sofa*'.

Plates 85–86.   PAUL GAUGUIN. '*The Wife of the King*'.

Plates 87–88.   H. DE TOULOUSE-LAUTREC. *Woman Adjusting her Stocking*.

Plates 89–90.   PIERRE BONNARD. 'Nude Dressing'.

Plates 91–92. HENRI MATISSE. *'Loulou'*.

Plates 93–94.   AMEDEO MODIGLIANI. 'Nude'.

Plates 95–96.   PABLO PICASSO. *'Nude in the Forest'*.

Plates 97–98.   MARCEL GROMAIRE. '*Les Lignes de la Main*'.

Plates 101–102. KAREL APPEL. '*Machteld*'.

JOHN BROPHY...

..."has as many talents as a cat has lives," wrote Frank O'Connor. Known primarily as a novelist, Mr. Brophy has seen four of his best sellers made into successful films: *Waterfront, Immortal Sergeant, Turn the Key Softly* and *The Day They Robbed the Bank of England,* starring respectively Richard Burton, Henry Fonda, Joan Collins and Peter O'Toole.

His reputation as a critic of art and other universal subjects stems particularly from three widely hailed books: *The Human Face, The Human Face Reconsidered* and *The Face in Western Art.* Not surprisingly, his writings have been translated into sixteen languages.

The Face of the Nude continues his informed, thought-provoking and entertaining discussions of concepts of the world of art.

COMMENTARIES

Plates 1–2.

UNKNOWN EGYPTIAN ARTIST. 18th Dynasty (c. 1400 B.C.) 'Dancing Girls.' Fresco?: detail. London: British Museum.

Although this decoration is more than 3000 years old it still gives an effect of spontaneity, as though fresh from the hand of the painter-draughtsman who was so confidently master of the technique of his day. Plate 1 is the only illustration in the book to reproduce a head larger than in the original, and this serves to show more clearly how modern this charming picture is in style and feeling. It obeys a convention which, not so long ago, many people found disturbing: the head and face are in profile but the eye and the eyebrow are depicted as if seen from the front. The Egyptians, we may be sure, knew that such a combination was impossible, but clearly they liked it, and many people now can see why. Broad contour lines, maintaining an even width, have been used by many modern artists from Manet to Gauguin, Van Dongen and Gromaire, and many women at the present day use similar dark strokes when 'making up' their own faces — not always with so pleasing an effect.

What tunes the musicians were playing we shall never know, but the two girls performing an acrobatic dance have a timeless grace. The decoration appears to have been done in pure fresco; that is to say, mineral pigments were used, mixed with water, and were applied to the plaster surface while it was still damp.

Plates 3–4.

UNKNOWN SCULPTOR. 6th Century B.C. 'Apollo of Tenea'. Stone. Munich: Glyptothek.

This famous statue in the Greek archaic style is named from where it was found, Tenea, not far from Corinth. It is presumed to represent Apollo, although some cautious scholars describe it merely as the figure of a youthful athlete. The unknown sculptor's aims were severely limited. almost certainly because he lacked the technical resources to attempt a more dynamic pose. One can imagine that such stiffly posed figures were first made by chipping away at a vertical rock face to make a carving in relief, and that it seemed a great advance when it was found possible to carve the back as well as the front of the face and body.

This Apollo has affinities with Egypt a thousand years earlier, in the stance and the general effect of flatness, and with Assyria and other Near Eastern countries where, like the written languages, faces were constructed largely of triangular forms and invested with an 'enigmatic' smile. Apollo was not only the God of the sun and of light but an ideal of masculine beauty. Here it looks as if were he to succeed in moving, it would be jerkily, and perhaps he is rather long in the neck — but cf. Plates 17 (Botticelli), 37 (Ammanati), and 97 (Gromaire).

Plates 5–6.

UNKNOWN HELLENISTIC SCULPTOR. 4th–2nd Century B.C. 'The Medici Venus'. Marble. Florence: Uffizi Gallery.

This figure takes its name from the Roman villa of the Medici family, where it stood until it was moved to Florence in the 17th century. Until recently it was regarded, along with such pieces as the Apollo Belvedere and the Venus of Cnidus, as an outstanding masterpiece of Classic Greek art. Nowadays it is depreciated, partly because it was overpraised not so long ago. The epithet 'Hellenistic', if strictly applied, would mean that it

is the work of someone who may have spoken Greek but was not himself a Greek. That, however, is more than we know, and the inscription on the base, which names the sculptor as 'Cleomanes, son of Apollodorus of Athens', is regarded by scholars as a misleading later addition. The statue was carried off to Paris as part of the enormous assembly of Napoleon's loot from conquered countries, and it was not returned until after Waterloo. (Cf. Plates 69–70, Canova).

Sir Kenneth Clark calls the Venus de Medici 'stilted and artificial', although he is careful to add that 'a number of good judges' have thought it 'a model of feminine beauty'. The pose is a variant of the 'Venus Pudica', which pose is said to express either modesty or shame in the sense of guilt — an emotion which, in view of the date of this and other sculptures, can hardly be passed off as the invention of Christianity. The head has at some time been removed and replaced, and the line of the right arm mars the rhythmic unity of that side of the body; this may be due to an error of judgment by one Ercole Ferrata who restored' the arms in the 17th century.

Plates 7–8.

UNKNOWN ARTIST IN POMPEII. 'Perseus and Andromeda'. Mural decoration. Naples: Museo Nazionale.

This splendid picture, buried to a depth of 20 feet when the city of Pompeii was overwhelmed by a volcanic eruption in A.D. 79, did not come to light again for more than 17 centuries. The artist was probably Roman, but as Pompeii, founded by Oscans, had at various times been under Greek and Etruscan domination before being conquered by Rome, there can be no certainty. The picture was found in the House of the Dioscuri (Castor and Pollux) which may indicate Greek associations; possibly we can see in this Perseus and Andromeda something of what Greek painting of the classical age, all of it now lost, must have looked like. At one time it was believed that the technique of such murals always involved the use of melted wax, but Professor A. P. Laurie makes a good case for fresco, applied to damp plaster, as described by Vitruvius and Pliny and apparently as used by the Egyptians 1500 years earlier. (Cf. Plate 2).

Perseus, who rescued Andromeda from a rock (here reduced to a merely symbolic size) to which she had been chained by a sea monster, was the child of Danaë by Zeus.

Plates 9–10.

UNKNOWN ROMAN ARTIST. 3rd–4th Century A.D. 'Girl Gymnasts'. Mosaic. Rome: Museo Nazionale Romano.

This is from a set of late Roman mosaics, recently excavated at Piazza Armerina in Sicily, and now to be seen at Rome in the museum housed in the ruins of the Baths of the Emperor Diocletian, close to the extremely 20th-century railway station. The girl is the centre figure of three, usually called gymnasts but perhaps better described as acrobats. The wheel fitted to a stick, which she holds in one hand, is presumably meant to be twirled, perhaps to distract the attention of the audience, as a conjuror does, or perhaps to maintain balance, as modern ropewalkers use a pole or an umbrella. Acrobatics (or 'tumbling') was a popular entertainment in the Ancient World — mural paintings in Crete show young men and girls turning somersaults over bulls' backs. This mosaic shows that the appeal was maintained in the later years of Imperial Rome. There is evidence that it lasted on through the Middle Ages, and it certainly survives today. The cloth which covers the breasts served a utilitarian purpose, but there is no reason to suppose that the fabric was elastic, although the effect is remarkably like that of a present day 'bikini' swimming costume.

Mosaics, of untraceably ancient origin, were used for decoration in most parts of the civilized world until the 13th century when fresco and tempera painting became more popular. The technique was to prepare small cubes of coloured, often gilded, stone, pottery, or glass and place them close together, according to a cartoon or other pattern, in a bed of cement. The result was extremely durable even when the mosaic was used for flooring instead of on a wall for purely decorative purposes. The name has nothing to do with Moses and the stone tablets of the Law, but comes, a little mysteriously, through Latin from the Greek word for the Muses.

Plates 11–12.
TILMAN RIEMENSCHNEIDER. 1460–1531. 'Eve'. Stone sculpture. Würzburg: Franconian Museum.

Riemenschneider is Gothic and belongs in style, if not in time, to the Late Middle Ages. He belongs also to the Renaissance, for he was contemporary with Dürer (compare Dürer's depiction of Eve in Plates 21–22) and only 15 years or so older than Michelangelo, with whom he had in common, so far as his works show, a temperamental disposition to take life very seriously. Both the grandeur and the dynamics of Michelangelo, however, were beyond Riemenschneider's scope. His sculpture, as here and in the companion piece, 'Adam', in the same museum, is poignant rather than tragic in effect. Carved about 1491–3, the two pieces are said to be the first adult nude figures, other than on crucifixes, in German sculpture.

Riemenschneider was a man of genuine piety and good will. He became mayor (burgomaster) of Würzburg and took the side of the landless and powerless in the Peasants' War of 1524–5. When he was captured he was subjected to torture. He was not only stretched on the rack, but his hands were crushed so that he could never work again.

Plates 13–14.
LUCA SIGNORELLI. c. 1441–1523. 'The Resurrection'. Fresco: detail. Orvieto: the Cathedral.

Orvieto, between Florence and Rome, is one of those hill towns of Italy which, chiefly because there is no suitable place for factories, retain a great deal of the appearance and the seclusion they must have had towards the end of the Middle Ages. Orvieto Cathedral is Gothic, with grotesque metal sculptures and several mosaics on the façade and, inside, a chapel frescoed by Signorelli. The frescoes constitute his masterwork and one of the great decorations of the early Renaissance. He was a pupil of Piero della Francesca. There are devils and damned souls in these frescoes, painted in purples and greens, administering and suffering tortures. This group of figures is from a more cheerful scene but it still reveals a gloominess of mind which is thought to be an effect of the puritanical preachings of Savonarola.

Signorelli was ahead of his time in his knowledge of anatomy and his ability to draw muscular bodies in violent action, but something mediaeval remains in his work, especially perhaps in the faces. Michelangelo, who belonged to a younger genera-

tion, may have derived some of his terribilità or intense seriousness from Signorelli's example.

Plates 15–16.
GREGOR ERHART. Died 1540. 'Mary Magdalene'. Stone sculpture. Paris: The Louvre.

This figure, also South German, was carved not very long after Riemenschneider's 'Eve' (Plates 11–12). The two provide an instructive contrast, both in the physique of the bodies and in the faces. The 'Eve' is comparatively narrow shouldered and thin shanked, which, together with the long, solemn oval shape of the face, gives it an overall Gothic look. The 'Mary Magdalene', despite the realistic painting of the eyes and mouth, seems to belong to a period when food was more plentiful, or at least more nourishing, and the broadness and flatness of the face is less a generalized 'Northern' characteristic than typically German. Erhart, who was born in Ulm and worked in Augsburg, seems here to have anticipated the art style of a much later period, the Baroque.

Where the forearm of Riemenschneider's 'Eve' would have been placed is not precisely determinable, but it would obviously have passed in front of the body leaving a blank space rather awkwardly filled by hanging hair. In the 'Mary Magdalene' the posing is more sophisticated, the tilt of the head balancing the slight swing of the hips. Although the hands, joined in prayer, are asymmetrically placed, the arms do not break the columnar unity of the torso and the hair is disposed ingeniously, if rather coyly.

Plates 17–18.
SANDRO BOTTICELLI. c. 1455–1510. 'The Birth of Venus'. Tempera: detail. Florence: Uffizi Gallery.

Botticelli can hardly be fitted into any category or 'school' except the large one of Florentine. His style and his outlook are all his own, and he left no disciples to carry on a tradition. Yet many will see him as an important stylistic link between the Middle Ages and the Early Renaissance. His figures are often Gothic, and his delineatory outlines, weaving patterns of curves, remind us of illuminated manuscripts. He is also a forerunner of the elegant Mannerism of Parmigianino and Primaticcio. An elaborate allegory can be read into this picture, reconciling the pagan myth of Aphrodite's being born, as a fully grown woman rising from the sea, with Christianity. Without benefit from the allegory, this has become one of the best-known paintings in the world, and most people are content to enjoy it as a brilliantly drawn design involving an exquisite choice and arrangement of colours.

The physique of Botticelli's Venus has often been judged faulty — she is at least a third taller than a real-life woman so narrow at shoulders and hips could be, without looking freakish. Her shape does not please everyone either; her ankles and feet are said to be clumsy, and the slope of her shoulders has been compared to the shape of a bottle of hock. In Botticelli's composition, however, she is right, she is perfect, and her face is probably the most admired of all the faces ever depicted in paint.

Plates 19–20.
LEONARDO DA VINCI. 1452–1519. 'Half-length portrait of an Unknown Woman'. Black chalk. Chantilly: Musée Condé.

Many things about this large drawing are controversial but not the fact that as a drawing it is of high quality and exercises a considerable fascination. It is obviously closely related to Leonardo and if not the work of his own hand must be by some artist, such as Boltraffio or Luini, who assimilated the Leonardo style very thoroughly. It has been called a study for the most famous of all Leonardo's paintings, the 'Mona Lisa' or 'La Gioconda' at the Louvre, but the face is thinner, the hair differently arranged, and the placing of the hands, although similar, is not the same. Even the viewpoint adopted by the artist differs between drawing and painting. For some tastes the Chantilly face is more beautiful than that in the painting. Mr. Michael Levey suggests that the drawing, if it was done in France, may have provided the idea for various half-length nude paintings of Diane de Poitiers and other 16th-century beauties. Cf. Plate 48 (Bunel).

The drawing is in fact a cartoon for an untraced painting. In Plate 19, where the head is shown the same size as in the drawing itself, lines of tiny holes made with a pin can be seen outlining the eyes, the nose, the mouth, and the coils of the hair. These pricks were made through the paper cartoon on to plaster (for fresco) or gesso (a kind of plaster) covering a canvas or panel. By joining together the transferred prick marks the artist obtained an outline drawing which he could use as a foundation for his projected picture.

Plates 21–22.
ALBRECHT DÜRER. 1471–1528. 'Eve'. Oil. Madrid: The Prado.

People today know more about art than the people of any previous generation. Even those who do not travel abroad are familiar with all the great masterpieces of painting through two interacting processes — colour photography and colour printing. Until about a century ago, however, the only way of reproducing paintings, frescoes, sculptures, and drawings was as monochrome prints. In the 15th and 16th centuries to be able to etch and engrave was thus to have a vast and international public which less-gifted artists could only envy. Most of Dürer's work consists of woodcuts and engravings, and it is largely because of this that he occupies so important a place in the history of art. He introduced Italian designs into Germany and disseminated his own Northern ideas south of the Alps. This fact perhaps obscures his work as a painter for which he was greatly admired, especially for his mastery of verisimilitude and illusion achieved with delicate strokes of a fine brush.

The Madrid 'Eve' is a strange picture. The young woman has something of the 'Gothic' Middle Ages about her — emphasised by the million-to-one chance of the leafy branch's concealing her 'shame' — and she is fullfaced in a quite German, non-Italian style. Yet the proportions of her body belong to elegant Mannerism, and it might even be held that the precarious placing of her feet would be more appropriate in a statuette of a figure poised on a ball — Dürer, we may remember, was the son of a goldsmith. The sloping shoulders may be compared to those of Botticelli's Venus (Plate 17).

Plates 23–24.
MICHELANGELO (Michelangelo Buonarotti). 1475–1564. 'Dawn' ('Aurora'). Marble Florence: The Medici Chapel.

The chapel Michelangelo designed with marble tombs for Giuliano and Lorenzo di Medici adjoins the church of San Lorenzo and is approached through a noisy market. As at the Sistine Chapel in Rome the interior frequently reverberates with the din set up by guides shouting competitively in various languages. There are therefore undoubted advantages in approaching Michelangelo's greatest works through reproductions like these rather than by a personal visit. In the uncompleted chapel, begun in 1524, two seated statues of the Medici princes face each other from opposite walls. Beneath each is a casket-like tomb surmounted by two reclining figures, one male, one female. One pair is known as Night and Day, the other as Dawn and Evening.

The Aurora figure expresses the very moment when sleep yields slowly to the demands of the coming day. The whole body is lax and heavy but without the reposefulness of the classical ideal. One feels that strength and abounding energy are stored in these marble limbs. The bending and lifting of the left arm, the outward curve of the hip, the upsurge of the knee, and the thrust downwards and away of the foot — as well as the long supple delineations of the extended right leg — all indicate why Michelangelo is accounted the first and greatest of the Mannerists.

Plates 25–26.
RAPHAEL (RAFFAELLO SANZIO). 1483–1520. 'The Triumph of Galatea'. Fresco. Rome: Villa Farnesina.

The Villa acquired its present name when it changed ownership 60 years after Raphael's death. It had been built for his patron, the banker Agostino Chigi, and was lavishly ornamented with mythological frescoes by Peruzzi, Giovanni da Udine, and others as well as Raphael. The story of Cupid and Psyche, spread over the ceiling of a long low room, follows Raphael's designs but is largely the work of his assistants, headed by Giulio Romano — Raphael, it is said, was too engrossed in a love affair to spare much time for the task. This Galatea fresco, however, in a nearby room, was painted by the master himself, in 1514, two or three years earlier. On the opposite wall another fresco (by Sebastiano del Piombo) shows Polyphemus singing love songs and Raphael's design incidentally illustrates her indifference to the Cyclops' wooing. Galatea was a nymph, one of the 50 daughters of Nereus, but like Thetis (see Plates 49–50, Cornelis van Haarlem) she had almost the status of a sea goddess.

While he was planning this fresco Raphael wrote in a letter, 'To paint one beautiful woman, I need to see several.' If, on this occasion, he did indeed use the eclectic method of combining features from various real-life models to form an idealized beauty, he was not very successful with the central figure of Galatea. In facial beauty, at least, she is eclipsed by one of her attendant nymphs, and this is the face that has been chosen for the detail plate.

Plates 27–28.
LUCAS CRANACH THE ELDER. 1472–1553. 'Venus and Cupid With The Stolen Honey'. Oil. London: National Gallery.

By comparison with Italian beauties in 16th-century paintings (cf. Plates 29, Titian; 31, Correggio; 33, Bronzino; 35, Salviati), this Venus may seem almost as spiky as a Gothic cathedral. Nevertheless she is the product of a comparatively late development in the career of Cranach, Court Painter to the Electors of Saxony, who — so far as is known — never visited Italy but yielded progressively to Italian influence in certain respects. The popularity of his nudes indicates that many Saxons of his day were glad to encourage their local art to step straight out of the mediaeval conventions into Mannerism.

The picture, acquired by the National Gallery only in 1963, shows Venus listening to the complaints of her son, Cupid, who has stolen a honeycomb and has been stung by the indignant bees. The subject is taken from a poem by Theocritus, and the Latin inscription draws a scolding moral for all of us. In body and in face the Venus undoubtedly represents a German ideal of feminine beauty of the period. Resplendent headdresses not unlike this one were worn. It looks also as though the eyebrows have been thinned by plucking, and almost certainly — the fashion was known in Italy — some head hair has been shaved or plucked out to make the forehead look higher.

Plates 29–30.
TITIAN (TIZIANO VECELLI). c. 1487 or 1490–1576. 'Danaë'. Oil. Naples: Museo Nazionale.

That Titian lived to be 99 is now considered unlikely. But his life was certainly long, and to the end, he was regarded as the greatest of all Venetian painters. Recently some art historians have seen in his late style with its free, almost slapdash application of paint to canvas, the true origin of modern painting technique. In this 'Danaë', however, which seems a superior composition to the other version of the same subject at Madrid, Titian is in his middle and most 'Titianesque' period. The design is full of classical repose and delicate balances, but there is no hint of that monumentality, akin to stone carving, to be found in some Mantegnas, or of those emphatic contour lines, as in Botticelli (Plates 17–18), Manet (Plates 79–80), and Matisse (Plates 91–92), which some critics object to as devices not 'painterly'. The colours are neither rich nor vivid, but they glow as if from below the surface — Titian is said to have done his underpainting in red earth and white lead pigments. The shapes and textures melt one into the other as voluptuously as the nude Danaë lies back on her pillows, while Zeus visits her in the guise of a shower of gold. The child born of this encounter was Perseus who slew Medusa and delivered Andromeda from the monster which kept her chained, naked, to a rock (cf. Plates 7–8, Pompeian mural painting).

Plates 31–32.
CORREGGIO (Antonio Allegri). c. 1494–1534. 'The Education of Cupid'. Oil. London: National Gallery.

Correggio, who takes his name from the place of his birth, is not so popular as he was during the 18th century when the charm, the pervasive air of gentleness, and the golden glow of his pictures appealed especially to those who found in the cult of 'sensibility' a delicacy of the emotions — refuge from the Age of Reason. Correggio still has a wide appeal and is seen now, like Mantegna and Piero della Francesca, as an artist of natural independence, a little apart from the fashions of his own time, and a forerunner of the Baroque. He worked chiefly in his native city and in nearby Parma. This picture was in the Gonzaga collection at Mantua in 1627, was bought for Charles I of England in 1628, and was sold off after the execution of the King. It went to Spain and in 1808 was seized by one of Napoleon's generals, Murat. In the year of Waterloo it was bought in Vienna by Lord Londonderry, who in 1834 sold it to the National Gallery.

The picture has survived all these vicissitudes remarkably well. It has gone under various names perhaps because no one knows exactly what instructions Mercury and Venus are giving to Cupid. It may be that they are teaching him his duties as a mischief-maker, but possibly they are teaching him, like any other small child, nothing more startling than the alphabet.

Plates 33–34.
BRONZINO (Agnolo di Cosimo). 1503–1572. 'Allegory'. Oil. London: National Gallery.

Venus and Cupid appear here also, but the meaning is not so clear or so simple as in the Correggio of Plate 31. Cupid is no longer a baby; he is almost adolescent, and his lover-like gesture towards his mother has seemed offensive to some critics, while Freudians have regarded it as an unintended but illuminating disclosure. The picture was undoubtedly designed to convey an allegorical meaning. Venus and Cupid are together taken as a symbol of sensual love, and the boy standing upright, with roses in his hands, is said to symbolize either Pleasure or Folly. The bald and bearded man who stretches his arms across the top of the picture represents Time, and the female whose head is seen at the top left corner has been read as Truth. These two are apparently figures of inevitable retribution, for the open-mouthed figure at the left, behind Cupid, is interpreted as Envy or Jealousy, and the monstrous creature with a girl's face, an animal's legs, and a serpent's tail is said to be Deceit.

The intention may be to moralize: the posing of the nude bodies and the porcelain-like depiction of bare skin, so characteristic of Bronzino, seems, however, to stultify the intention. The picture is as Florentine as the Correggio is Parmesan but in a very sophisticated fashion indeed.

Plates 35–36.
FRANCESCO SALVIATI. 1510–1563. 'Charity' ('La Carità'). Oil. Florence: Uffizi Gallery.

Salviati had an international reputation in his own lifetime and was invited to follow Rosso and Primaticcio to France. Since then he has been half-neglected by critics and is only now beginning to be studied thoroughly as one of the most gifted of the Florentine Mannerists. Like Parmigianino he was by nature an experimental draughtsman, and his drawings are numerous and varied in style. As might be expected, therefore, the best of his larger work was done in fresco, and while his frescoes in Rome (at the Palazzo Farnese and the Palazzo Sacchetti) are difficult of access, there is on an upper floor of the Palazzo Vecchio in Florence, open to everyone almost every day, the graceful and exciting Camillo series.

At the Uffizi nearby can be seen this large painting in oil which, with its firm and unstrained composition, its clear colours and simple poses, makes such a striking contrast with the work of more sophisticated Mannerists such as Bronzino (cf. Plate 33). There is symbolism here but no allegory, and the Charity depicted is the Pauline virtue, the one that excels both Faith and Hope.

Plates 37–38.
BARTOLOMEO AMMANATI. 1511—1592. 'A Sea Goddess'. Bronze. Florence: Piazza della Signoria.

Ammanati designed the Neptune fountain that stands at one side of the square, close to the Palazzo Vecchio, and although it is not certain that he designed each one of the bronze figures grouped round the outer rim of the basin, no other author is known. This superb open-air bronze is, therefore, credited to him. The style is elegant Mannerist, and the head is a little narrower, the limbs a little more tapering, than in Michelangelo's marble 'Aurora' (Plate 23) only a mile or so away. Ammanati was a successful architect — he redesigned the front of the Pitti Palace — whose sculpture is at least comparable with that of the better-known Giovanni da Bologna.

In his old age, Ammanati developed a bad conscience about the nude figures he had modelled in the days of his youth, and in 1582 addressed a sort of open letter to 'my dearest brethren of the Florentine Academy' beseeching them 'never to make anywhere any work which is indecent or lewd — I am referring to completely unclothed figures — nor anything else which may move any man or woman, of any age, to wicked thoughts.' About eight years later he begged the Grand Duke Ferdinand for permission to work on his sculptures in the Boboli Gardens and 'clothe them artistically and decently, re-naming them after various virtues.' Those figures, however, like those on the Neptune fountain, are still nude and no one seems any the worse because of it.

Plates 39–40.
TINTORETTO (Jacopo Robusti). 1518–1594. 'Susanna and the Elders'. Oil. Vienna: Kunsthistorisches Museum.

Some of the beauties in Venetian paintings have the plump, languorous look of odalisques, as if the long commerce with Turkey had orientalized Venetian taste. Tintoretto's Susanna, however, admiring herself beside her garden bathing pool and unaware that the lecherous elders are also admiring her, can hardly be thought Oriental. She is plump — almost plump enough to be in a Rubens picture — but her blond hair is braided in classical — Greek or Roman — style, and her face makes one think of Verrocchio, Salviati, and other Florentines. Salviati (Plate 35) came to Venice to paint frescoes — now lost — at the Palazzo Grimani when Tintoretto was only 21, and the young Venetian, already an independent artist, must have been greatly stimulated and influenced.

Michelangelo, although known only through engravings, drawings, and small-scale clay models, is another formative influence discernible in Tintoretto's compositions. Here the great Venetian shows how subtle and sound his designing skill could be by making a perfect counterbalance between the underlying angularities of Susanna's pose and the undulatory outlines of her figure.

Plates 41–42.
EL GRECO (Domenikos Theotocopoulos). 1541–1614. 'Laocoön'. Oil. Washington D.C.: National Gallery of Art, Samuel H. Kress collection.

Laocoön is one of those unfortunates in Greek legend who underwent a fearful punishment because they displeased the gods. Apollo, whose priest he was, took offence when Laocoön warned the besieged Trojans not to admit to the city a huge horse, made of wood, in which Greek soldiers were concealed. A pair of snakelike monsters emerged from the sea and, coiling round Laocoön and his two sons, slowly crushed them to death. The story is told by Virgil in the Aeneid, and was made especially vivid to 16th-century Italians by a large and much-admired piece of Greek sculpture (now in the Vatican) discovered in Rome in 1506.

El Greco came from his native Crete to Venice, where his style was influenced by Tintoretto, and later made his name in Spain. Most of his work is religious and mystical. This unusual picture is mythological in subject but may have mystical significances no longer clear to us. The two (or three) figures at the right are unexplained, unless one of them represents Apollo. El Greco ranks with Van Gogh as one of the great neurotics of art, endowed with a bizarre vision all his own. The composition is Mannerist not only in the elongated shapes of bodies and limbs, but in the angular postures for which precedents can be found in Michelangelo's Sistine Chapel frescoes.

Plates 43–44.
SCHOOL OF FONTAINEBLEAU. 16th Century. 'Diana Goddess of the Chase'. Oil. Paris: The Louvre.

The Greek Artemis — the Roman Diana — retains something of the Near-Eastern conception of a Moon Goddess, and here, as in many Renaissance and post-Renaissance pictures, this association is indicated by a small crescent worn in the hair. It is almost a totem sign. The other aspect of Diana, as the presiding deity of hunting, with bow and arrow and attendant hounds, is more often exploited by painters. Along with the desire to chase and kill animals goes — rather oddly one would think — a temperamental chastity, contrasted with the amorous dispositions of other goddesses, notably Venus. In art Diana is traditionally fair haired, pale skinned, with small breasts set high. Her chastity is paradoxically hot-tempered; she likes to go naked but when by chance a man, Actaeon, sees her bathing she magically changes him into a stag — presumably so that he can be hunted and killed either by the hounds or by a shot from the goddess' bow.

This is one of the most beautiful of Diana pictures, simple, hardly Mannerist at all, constructed around the intersection of a vertical and horizontal, and serene — indeed the goddess looks to be rather a dreamer. It is presumably associated with the Palace of Fontainebleau but may be the work of a transplanted Italian; the face reminds one a little of Luini (cf. Plate 19, Leonardo), but both the trees and the intricate folding of the flying robe suggest Niccolo dell' Abbate.

Plates 45–46.
PAOLO CALIARI VERONESE. 1528–88. 'Venus and Mars'. Oil. Turin: Pinacoteca (Sabauda Gallery).

Venus occurs as an idealization of natural love and physical beauty in many of the pictorial themes — taken from Greek and Latin myths so far as they were then known and understood — of the Renaissance and later periods. She is born, adult, from the sea (Plates 17–18, Botticelli); she is seen in her material function with Cupid (Plates 27–28, Cranach; 31–32, Correggio), and at her toilet (Plates 63–64, Boucher). She carries off the prize for supreme beauty in the 'Judgment of Paris' (Plates 49–50, Cornelis van Haarlem) and is involved in various amours — principally with the youth Adonis, destined to be killed by a boar (Plates 51–52, Carracci), and Mars, the God of War. Mars was caught with her in a net by the indignant Vulcan who then displayed the guilty pair to the other deities.

Veronese, that persuasive advocate of a *dolce vita* all apparently fun and feasts, has interrupted the lovers at a critical moment when the war god's horse, tethered outside, has grown either impatient or inquisitive. There is a variant of this picture in the Metropolitan Museum, New York, in which the scene is set outdoors; two cupids are in attendance, and the horse looks so scandalized that he might almost be Vulcan.

Plates 47–48.
FRANÇOIS BUNEL THE YOUNGER. 1552–1595. '*A Lady at her Toilet*'. Oil. Dijon: Musée des Beaux-Arts.

In 16th-century France there was a fashion among royal mistresses and other ladies of less-than-perfect virtue for having themselves painted naked. Gabrielle d'Estrées (who at least once was painted with her sister, also stripped, beside her) seems to have set the fashion. Some semblance of modesty was preserved by concealing the lower part of the body in a bath, much as in many ancient statues of Venus everything below the waist was draped. This picture shows the top of a dressing-table being used for the same concealing purpose.

Nobody knows with absolute certainty who the sitter was or who painted the picture. It was attributed to Bunel when it was exhibited at the Rijksmuseum, Amsterdam, in 1955, and this seems more likely than attributions to Franz Floris or Pourbus. Bunel, born in Blois, became a court painter to Henry de Navarre, afterwards Henry IV, but this picture must be earlier. It is in all probability a portrait of Diane de Poitiers, Duchesse d'Anet and mistress of Henry II. It corresponds closely and in detail — shoulders, breasts, arms, hands, head, and hair — to the 'Diane au Cerf' sculpture at the Louvre, which came from her own chateau at Anet, and the face, although less idealized than in the sculpture, is clearly recognizable.

Plates 49–50.
CORNELIS CORNELISZ VAN HAARLEM. 1562–1628. '*The Wedding of Peleus and Thetis*'. Oil. Haarlem: Frans Hals Museum.

Peleus was king of the Myrmidones in Thessaly. His wedding — he is the one who holds a goblet of wine in one hand and lays the other on his bride's shoulder — was an imaginary but momentous event that links together Greek history, Greek myth, and Greek poetry. He married Thetis, a sea or water nymph, and neglected to invite a certain goddess, Eris, who presided over discord, to the wedding feast. Resenting this, Eris sent an apple with the inscription 'For the most beautiful'. Three goddesses, Venus, Juno, and Minerva, claimed the honour, and a shepherd named Paris was appointed to judge between their claims. He gave the apple to Venus (this is the scene depicted on a hilltop in the background), and as a reward Venus promised him a woman as beautiful as herself — Helen, daughter of Leda and Zeus. Helen was already married to a Greek, Menelaus, and when Paris carried her off to Troy the Greeks went to war to recapture her. Thetis bore Peleus a son, Achilles, who became the hero, on the Greek side, of the Trojan war, which is the subject of Homer's 'Iliad'.

This painting, late Northern Mannerist in style, is by one of the lesser known but highly gifted Dutch artists, contemporary with Goltzius but also with Rubens. As in many pictures from the Netherlands and northern France, some of the faces are Celtic in colouring and shape and with a distinctive look of wide-eyed unsophistication. Thetis (Plate 49) might be an Irish or Scottish farm girl, while some will see in her rounded face a distinct resemblance to the Welsh poet Dylan Thomas in his youth.

Plates 51–52.
ANNIBALE CARRACCI. 1560–1609. '*Adonis meets Venus*'. Oil. Vienna: Kunsthistorisches Museum.

Annibale Carracci, a more important artist than his cousin Ludovico or his brother Agostino, was head of a busy studio and the chief exponent of a style, at one time called Eclectic, associated with Bologna and with a revolt against Mannerism — or at least against Mannerism in its Roman decline — at the end of the 16th century. It is true that Carracci stands, in general terms, not only for academic drawing as a foundation for picture making but for repose, true-to-life proportions in the human figure, and the avoidance of extravagant attitudes, but such classic principles were not repudiated by all Mannerists. Some of Annibale Carracci's paintings and drawings have Mannerist qualities; some are as realistic as the rendering of the doves and the dog's head here. This picture shows Annibale painting as though he came from Bologna and had studied Correggio (Plates 31–32), although some people see Venetian characteristics and the influence of Titian (Plates 29–30) in it, especially in the face of Venus. He visited both cities.

The story of Venus and Adonis is a tragic idyll. The goddess of love, stimulated by an arrow from Cupid's bow, fell in love with a handsome youth she encountered in a forest. He preferred to get on with his hunting and was killed by the wild boar he sought to slay. From his blood, red anemones are said to have sprung.

Plates 53–54.
JOOS VAN WINGHE. 1544–1603. '*Apelles and Campaspe*'. Oil. Vienna: Kunsthistorisches Museum.

Apelles of Ephesus was considered the greatest painter of his time — the 4th century B.C. — and especially admired for his graceful compositions and his skill with the brush. Alexander the Great gave him an official appointment as portrait painter, and one of his commissions was to make a nude portrait of Campaspe, Alexander's mistress. A legend, clearly designed to exemplify the monarch's largeness of heart, has it that when Alexander observed that Apelles and Campaspe were falling in love with each other he released his beautiful mistress from her obligations to himself and allowed her to live happily with the painter.

This flattering story, told by Pliny, was popular with painters and from the 16th century became a stock subject for pictures. It was perhaps not so popular with patrons who may have felt they were cast in the background role of Alexander. Joos van Winghe, born in Brussels, is one of the lesser-known of the Netherlandish-Italianate Mannerists. He spent four years in Italy before settling down in Frankfurt. After his death this picture belonged to the Emperor Rudolf II, one of the great collectors of Mannerist art. There is another version at Vienna, which once belonged to the Duke of Buckingham, with considerable differences in the pose and other details.

Plates 55–56.
SIR PETER PAUL RUBENS. 1577–1640. '*The Daughters of Leucippus Seized by Castor and Pollux*'. Oil. Munich: Pinakothek.

The two women in this picture (who seem startled but hardly dismayed by what is happening to them) are characteristic Rubens nudes painted characteristically. Their vigorous health and plumpness may be contrasted with the leaner look of Riemenschneider's 'Eve' (Plate 11) and even with Botticelli's 'Venus' (Plate 17). The difference may be due to the fact that by the end of the 16th century, people were much better fed, and those who could afford it tended to eat too much. Rubens was an international figure, in great demand not only in his native Flanders, but in London, Paris, Rome, and Madrid. The picture is a truly Baroque composition, a unified complexity balancing a number of vigorous movements against each other with a total effect of undoubted grandeur. With other Baroque painters of the period the total effect is apt to be grandiose and displeasing to many people. Rubens' advantage over such painters as Maratta, Guido Reni, and Lebrun is partly technical, in the handling of the brush and in drawing, and partly temperamental: the people he paints may be stylized but they are not idealized; they convey a marvellous illusion of reality to the eye. He probably excelled all other artists in suggesting in paint the mantling of blood beneath the skin.

Castor and Pollux are an odd couple even for classical myth. They were brothers, and may have been twins, children of Leda, one by Zeus in the guise of a swan, one by a human father, and hatched from an egg, or from two eggs. When they reached manhood they joined forces to seize brides for themselves. Unfortunately, the brides were intended for other bridegrooms who, not surprisingly, made a fuss about it.

Plates 57–58.
JACOB JORDAENS. 1593–1678. *Pan and Syrinx*. Oil. Brussels: Musée des Beaux-Arts.

Metamorphosis — physical change carried out instantly and to an extreme, so that a human being retains mind and spirit and individuality although turned into the body of an animal or a tree — occurs frequently in ancient myths and persists in the fairy stories of modern times. Its psychological significance is probably occult and complex. When Apollo pursued the nymph Daphne she appealed to her father, a river god, who used his magical powers to metamorphose her into a laurel bush. The story of Pan and Syrinx is of the same order except that Syrinx went in for self-help. To save her chastity she turned herself into a reed. It is perhaps an over-fanciful embellishment of the story which makes the goat-legged, lustful god fashion 'the pipes of Pan' out of the reed, although some will see in it an early unconscious acknowledgement that art may be, in origin, a by-product of thwarted sexual desire.

Jordaens is coarser, less skilful, and less imaginative than Rubens, to whom he was chief assistant and in many ways chief successor. He was nonetheless a considerable artist and, because he was so little under Italian influence, he makes an excellent representative of the time and place in which he lived, as non-classical and non-aristocratic as Rembrandt. The model for Syrinx was probably his wife, and her body is so pale that we may guess she posed in winter with a white towel or sheet around her and a blazing fire not far away.

Plates 59–60.
REMBRANDT VAN RIJN. 1606–1669. *Bathsheba*. Oil. Paris: The Louvre.

Bathsheba was the wife of Uriah the Hittite, and when David saw her — from the roof of his palace — while she was bathing, he desired her. He sent her a letter proposing a liaison, to which Bathsheba agreed. David went further and, as if he had been a Chicago gangster in the 1920s, arranged for Uriah to be killed in battle. For this God punished him: his child by Bathsheba died. Later she bore David another child, Solomon, who eventually succeeded him as King of Israel. Rembrandt has depicted the moment of choice on which this romantic and tragic story depends — the moment when Bathsheba has received the royal letter and is about to yield to the flattering temptation. There are deliberate ironies in the picture, which was painted in 1654. The model for Bathsheba was Hendrickje Stoffels, the young maid-servant who, after the death of his wife, Rembrandt made his mistress. Hendrickje had just borne him a child which, like Bathsheba's, died while still a baby.

The picture may be compared with Titian's 'Danaë' (Plate 29) as examples of Italian and Northern treatment of the nude, but although the Titian has a pagan theme and the face of his Danaë has little character when matched against Rembrandt's pensive Bathsheba, the two pictures are — perhaps surprisingly — quite similar in the way they make the nude female body an evocation of golden light out of surrounding darkness.

Plates 61–62.
GIOVANNI BATTISTA TIEPOLO. 1696–1770. 'America'. Fresco. Würzburg (Franconia, Germany): Residenz Museum.

Tiepolo, now recognized by many as the greatest decorative painter of the Baroque and Rococo periods, excelling Pietro da Cortona, Boucher, and — some would say — Annibale Carracci, belongs, like Guardi and Canaletto, to the final, the sunset episode of Venetian painting when the focus of the visual arts was no longer on anywhere in Italy but on Paris. Tiepolo worked hard through a long life and left behind him a large number of paintings, some finished works, others try-out sketches on a small scale, and a vast number of superb drawings. Nevertheless, from soon after his death until the early years of the 20th century his reputation was in eclipse. He was hardly known, for about 120 years, to those people who consider themselves reasonably well informed about art, and critics either dismissed him as a minor late Venetian or abused him for the extravagance of his imagination. This is hard to believe nowadays when reproductions of his splendid, colourful, and exhilarating compositions have made him immensely popular, but taste plays some very strange tricks: Botticelli was virtually forgotten, in Italy as well as elsewhere, for three whole centuries.

There are splendid works by Tiepolo in his native Venice, but the greatest of all lies off the main tourist routes — the vast ceilings of the elegant building at Würzburg which once was the palace of the Prince-Archbishop. In some ways these are the most impressive frescoes ever made. This is one of hundreds of allegorical or historical figures, painted just half way through the 18th century, when already the Red-Indian head-dress of coloured feathers had become internationally recognizable as a symbol of the American continent.

Plates 63–64.
FRANÇOIS BOUCHER. 1703–1770. *The Toilet of Venus*. Oil. Paris: The Louvre.

The subject was a favourite one with many painters, as it permits a beautiful nude to be shown, indoors and outdoors, with jewels, combs, rich cloths, and other ornamental accessories including the amorous doves always associated with Venus. For this version Boucher ingeniously arranges his composition into an irregular pyramid set off by triangular shapes above and below. The model is Maria Louise O'Morphi who was one of the concubines of Louis XV, perhaps the most loved of them — not that the Bien-Aimé's love amounted to much more than a jaded appetite — and certainly the best known to posterity. Boucher painted her often as a naked nymph or goddess from soon after she was installed, at the age of 15, in the Parc-aux-Cerfs at Versailles. Here she is a little older, and her face has lost some of its baby-like chubbiness, taking on a characteristically Celtic look (cf. Plate 49, Cornelis van Haarlem), for her name is often spelled Murphy, and both her parents came from Dublin.

Boucher in his later years shocked Sir Joshua Reynolds by confessing that he often painted nudes from memory. In 'The Toilet of Venus', however, we can assume that he not only made preliminary drawings but painted with Louise in front of him; the former royal mistress, Madame de Pompadour, perhaps acted as chaperon. 'La Belle O'Morphi' afterwards had three husbands in succession, was imprisoned during the Revolution, and died, at the age of 77, as late as 1814 — just before Napoleon escaped from Elba and headed for Waterloo.

Plates 65–66.
THOMAS GAINSBOROUGH. 1727–1788. *Musidora*. Oil. London: Tate Gallery.

Gainsborough has three reputations: as a portraitist, as a landscape painter, and as a draughtsman, especially in black chalk. His portraits won him fame and fortune during his lifetime, and, at the end of the 19th century and the opening of the 20th, such pictures as 'The Blue Boy' fetched tremendously high prices. His own first and abiding interest was in landscape and in drawings made of farms and woodlands, often including cottagers and their children. It is for these that he is most esteemed today.

Gainsborough was as rural as Fragonard (cf. Plates 67–68) and in fact spent much more of his time in the countryside. His subjects include few love scenes, and, by comparison with Fragonard, he is less down to earth, more 'poetic' — or perhaps the difference is much the same as between French and English poetry. 'Musidora' shows him in an Arcadian mood and indicates that, in treating the nude, reticence has certain advantages. The brushwork in some ways anticipates Impressionist techniques of the following century. 'Musidora' was painted during the last decade of his life, and it is possible that Emma Hamilton, Nelson's mistress, was the model.

Plates 67–68.
JEAN-HONORÉ FRAGONARD. 1732–1806. *Girls Bathing* ('Les Baigneuses'). Oil: detail. Paris: The Louvre.

Fragonard spent five years, during his twenties, studying in Rome, but it would not be easy to show that either the ancient monuments or the paintings and sculptures of the Renaissance had much effect on his art. He was a Paris painter who supplied the wealthier aristocracy with frivolously idyllic pictures of contemporary love scenes. A pupil of Boucher (cf. Plates 63–

64), he at first rivalled him, then succeeded him, as a fashionable artist whose compositions were widely popularized through engravings.

He was also — though only briefly — a pupil of Chardin, and there is some significance in this, for there runs through Fragonard's work a strain of simplicity and directness. He was less urban than Boucher, more of a countryman in outlook. A Southerner — he was born in Grasse — he makes his lovers and nymphs look not only a trifle rustic but as though they had been out in hot sunshine and enjoyed it. The girls in 'Les Baigneuses' are playing like puppy dogs, yet the picture is not wholly naturalistic: the girl with the flowers in her hand floats on the air like an allegorical personage on a palace ceiling. The moral or message of the picture, however, if it has one, is merely that life can be enjoyable.

Plates 69–70.
ANTONIO CANOVA. 1757–1822. *Venus Victorious*. Marble. Rome: Borghese Gallery.

This remarkable sculpture in the Neo-Classic style is often called, even in official publications, by the name of the model, Pauline Bonaparte, sister of the Emperor. She might not perhaps have been considered a great beauty but for her membership in the Corsican family which, for a time, outshone all the royal dynasties of Europe except those of Britain and Russia. She was a leader of fashion under the Directory and the Empire and was notorious for her love affairs. Not only the dressing of her hair and her pose but the draping of the lower part of her body in this, the best known of all Canova's marbles, has classical precedents. She married, at the age of 17, one of Napoleon's generals. He died in 1802, and the next year she married a Roman, Prince Camillo Borghese. It was five years later, when she was 28, that she sat for the Venetian sculptor, Canova. The 'Venere Vincitrice' is exhibited in the palace formerly belonging to her husband's family.

Canova's sculpture is too plastic to satisfy every taste. Marble, when he has finished with it, looks as if it had been modelled in soft clay rather than carved. The figure, nevertheless, has both grace and dignity. After Waterloo, Canova played a leading part in recovering for Italy many of the art treasures looted by Napoleon. Pauline died comparatively young, in 1825.

Plates 71–72.
JEAN BAPTISTE REGNAULT. 1754–1829. *The Three Graces*. Oil. Paris: The Louvre.

Regnault was a Member of the Academy of the Fine Arts and held a professorial chair. He was the sort of painter who conforms easily to the social and artistic conventions of his own time, is regarded as 'eminent' and 'distinguished' while he lives — and sinks into oblivion almost as soon as he dies. This process of rise and fall in reputation is, possibly, inevitable, but it is often unjust. Academic artists are depreciated because they bring little or no novelty to the development of art, yet the novelty on which many reputations are founded is necessarily ephemeral. Once it has been accepted it is no longer novel.

'The Three Graces' reveals how good a picture an academic artist working on a well-worn subject can produce. Groups of the *charités* standing with linked arms, sometimes as if dancing in a circle, are common in Greek and Roman art and from the Renaissance onwards. There is a small, exquisite painting by Raphael at Chantilly; Botticelli incorporated the Graces with the 'Primavera'; Tintoretto, the Carracci, Rubens, and Goltzius all found the subject attractive. By tradition, the group is always so arranged that it affords one front, one back and one side view of the female nude, as here, or alternatively two front views and one back view.

Plates 73–74.
JEAN AUGUSTE DOMINIQUE INGRES. 1780–1867. *'The Spring'* (*'La Source'*). Oil. Paris: The Louvre.

The Romans, the Renaissance painters, and the Mannerists sometimes depicted naiads but on the whole preferred to personify flowing water as a bearded and burly river god. Later, an alternative came into favour, and a naked young woman standing upright and pouring water from an urn or pitcher was especially popular with French artists. This is the best known of all 'La Source' paintings. It shows what principles Ingres stood for as leader of the academic, classical school at the opposite pole, in temperament and in technique, to the Romantics. The composition binds within itself all suggestions of physical exertion and movement, so that the overall effect is of repose and serenity. Careful drawings, establishing proportion, modelling, and placings within the picture, have preceded the actual painting. The colours are chosen to suggest coolness, and the smooth paint is thin enough for the weave of the canvas to show through at a close inspection. The forearms, the curves of the pitcher, the outward swing of the hip, and the bent leg provide visual reliefs from the dominant verticals of the composition.

Almost everybody finds something to like in this picture, whether or not the girl's face is judged to be lacking in character and expression. Her figure has almost the slender elongations of a Parmigianino, and this perhaps is an indirect consequence of the revival of Mannerism by two painters — Fuseli and Géricault — with whom Ingres otherwise had little in common.

Plates 75–76.
EUGÈNE DELACROIX. 1798–1863. *'The Death of Sardanapalus'.* Oil. Paris: The Louvre.

Sardanapalus was a legendary tyrant probably identical with Assur-bani-pal, a 7th-century B.C. king of Assyria. Byron wrote a poetical drama about him, and Delacroix, always interested in things English, derived from it the idea of this huge painting. The tyrant, with his palace besieged by rebels, prefers to die rather than to be captured. First, however, he orders his wives and concubines to be slain on the property owner's principle, 'If I can't have her, no one else shall!'. This is the chief group in the foreground of a picture crowded not only with figures in vigorous action but with jewellery, goblets, rich cloths, and a white horse. The colours are vivid and rich, and the paint has been applied skilfully but often as if in response to a sudden impulse.

Delacroix made many preliminary drawings for 'The Death of Sardanapalus', and the composition was certainly not improvised. The picture is nevertheless typical of the early 19th-century Romantic movement, which, one can see, owed a good deal to dynamic Mannerism but defied its constructional dis-

ciplines. The contrast with the cool colours and the composure of the Ingres 'La Source' (Plate 73) is striking.

Plates 77–78.
GUSTAVE COURBET. 1819–1877. *'The Woman With a Parrot'.* Oil. New York: Metropolitan Museum of Art, Bequest of Mrs. H. O. Havemeyer, 1929, The H. O. Havemeyer Collection.

This is an example of the third 'school' or movement in French art of the first half of the 19th century — Realism. Courbet was intent on depicting things not as he saw them but as he knew them to be; in this respect he can be compared with the Pre-Raphaelites and with other, more academic painters in many European countries. In France he stands between the Classical school, led by Ingres, which he repudiated because he thought that it looked at life through idealistic, 'rose-coloured' spectacles, and the Romantic school, led by Delacroix, which he repudiated as unreal and literary. He held strong political opinions and could be accused of many prejudices. He was imprisoned and fined for inciting the mob to pull down the column in the Place Vendôme.

This nude, done in 1866, provides some illuminating comparisons with the Delacroix of Plates 75–76, which was painted 37 years earlier. While the flesh tints differ considerably, the faces are so similar that one wonders if the Delacroix model could have been grandmother to the girl who sat for Courbet. In certain respects the picture is romantic; it is also a carefully arranged and idealized report on naked female beauty, and it is possible that Courbet had more in common with Ingres and Delacroix than he realized.

Plates 79–80.
EDOUARD MANET. 1832–1883. *'Déjeuner sur l'herbe'* (*'The Picnic'*). Oil. Paris: The Louvre.

This picture was rejected in 1862, when Manet was 30 years old, for the annual exhibition best known as 'the Salon'. Manet, to whom the social standards of fashionable Paris were important, was offended and surprised. It must have been obvious to him, however, that to depict two fully dressed young men in the open air accompanied by two young women, one quite naked, with her clothes thrown aside on the grass, was asking for trouble. The argument that the picture should have been accepted because other painters in the past, notably Giorgione and Titian, had similarly mixed nudes and fully clad figures in the same picture is fallacious. Neither the Giorgiones nor the Titians were, so far as we know, put on public exhibition while the artists were still alive.

The nude model was Victorine Meurend. In 1865 Manet had a painting of her, nude, accepted and shown at the Salon. It was called 'Olympia'; it was set indoors and there were no men in it. Victorine Meurend was again the model, and the picture incensed the visiting public so much that it had to be hung higher, out of reach. Manet may have been one of Victorine's lovers; there is a story that when she was old and destitute she applied to Manet's widow for assistance but was turned away from the door.

Plates 81–82.
EDGAR-HILAIRE-GERMAINE DEGAS. 1834–1917. *'After the Bath'.* Pastels. Paris: Collection Durand-Ruel. © Sabam, Brussels; Spadem, Paris.

Degas was an odd and apparently irascible character, argumentative but, unlike Cézanne, pragmatic rather than doctrinaire in his views of art. He was associated with both Impressionists and Post-Impressionists, but his most important work, done after he reached the age of 40, is in pastels. A pastel is a stick of chalk, the particles bound together with a little size, and a picture done in pastels is a drawing in colour. Degas therefore is hardly an Impressionist at all. He belongs to a line of delineating artists that includes Botticelli, Michelangelo, Tintoretto, and Ingres, and has since been continued by Toulouse-Lautrec, Matisse, and Picasso.

His pastels have a universal popularity, and of his three favourite subjects — ballet dancers, laundresses at work, and women at the bath — the third is perhaps the one that makes the greatest demand on his skill as a draughtsman and a colourist. Usually Degas arranged the pose — in his own studio where he provided bathtub, sponge, towels, and (sometimes) soap and water — so that the face was turned away or was in heavy shadow. This, which some consider the most beautiful of all the bathtub pastels, is a notable exception. By a strange coincidence the face of the unknown model bears quite a resemblance to the face in Gainsborough's 'Musidora' (Plates 65–66), for which the model is thought to have been Lady Hamilton.

Plates 83–84.
PIERRE-AUGUSTE RENOIR. 1841–1919. 'Nude on a Sofa'. Oil. Moscow: Pushkin Museum. © Sabam, Brussels; Spadem, Paris.

Renoir suffered many physical disabilities towards the end of his long life, and at all times his work is liable to vary considerably in quality. Because of the high reputation rightly earned by his best paintings, inferior work among his huge output commands extravagantly high prices and is to be found not only in the homes of rich men who lack discrimination but in many public galleries on both sides of the Atlantic. It is important therefore that the popular 'image' of Renoir should be founded on such brilliant and satisfying works as this. Here delineation is reduced to a minimum, and the nude body of a plump young woman is conveyed to our eyes as a genuinely 'Impressionist' experience, apparently instantaneous, vivid with light and colour but not precisely defined. The colour range is deliberately kept narrow: against the almost abstract background, dominated by blues, the creams and browns and greens of the flesh tones indicate the form of the nude body without emphasis on either shapes or posture.

The composition is built of underlying triangles (cf. Plates 39–40, Tintoretto), composed into one major triangle which supports the head and throws all the most powerful emphasis of the picture on the face. By making the lips comparatively red and adding the gold ear drop, Renoir heightens this emphasis even while, with the bright blues in the eyes and the hair, he prevents the figure from being merely a detached silhouette against the blue background and so unifies the whole composition.

Plates 85–86.
PAUL GAUGUIN. 1848–1903. 'The Wife of the King'. Oil. Moscow: Pushkin Museum.

Gauguin, who began as a 'Sunday' or spare-time painter and ended his life as a voluntary exile to Tahiti, is another Impressionist whose practise by no means accords with the theory of Impressionism. Neither Monet nor Renoir seems to

have liked his Tahiti pictures at all, and Pissarro thought he was making himself a savage. Degas saw merit in the pictures — but Degas himself was only nominally an Impressionist. Gauguin claimed the right to use colours arbitrarily, as he pleased, and described his pictures as "arrangements of lines and colours" with little or no relation to actuality. Tahitian subjects certainly afforded him great freedom of choice, for not one European in a million would have any idea whether his fruits and flowers and leaves were coloured as in nature or not. Apart from colour, the pictures are representational enough and, although the forms, like the perspective and modelling, are simplified, they are delineated with firm strokes of a brush loaded with dark paint. The result is a rare combination of skilful drawing and bold colouring. Gauguin ran away from Europe, but he could not escape from a European tradition of representational pattern-making traceable through 15th- and 16th-century Italian frescoists, such as Piero della Francesca and Uccello, back to the Romans and the Greeks.

Plates 87–88.
HENRI DE TOULOUSE-LAUTREC. 1864–1901. 'Woman Adjusting her Stocking'. Gouache and oil. Albi (France): Museum.

Born into the French aristocracy, Lautrec was apparently destined to lead the same sort of life as his father, staving off the boredom of too much leisure with blood sports and cultivating a few minor eccentricities as well as the privileges of rank and property. An accident that broke both his legs in childhood changed the programme: he grew up a grotesque dwarf; even his face seems to have been distorted by illness. Frustration and anger sent him to Paris, where he could cultivate his gift for drawing, but where he became a drunkard, passing from the comparatively respectable society of music-hall, café, and dance-hall entertainers to that of pimps and prostitutes, until, after a mental and physical collapse, he died at the age of 37.

This sketch, almost certainly executed in a brothel in 1894, admirably illustrates his style, his temperament, and his technique. Much more a draughtsman than a painter, Lautrec adds colour only when he has indicated shapes by means of line. His temperament is apparently realist, but perhaps it is by force of circumstance that he seeks out sordid subjects. Most people find his work powerfully romantic; it evokes not only the sense of beauty but also emotional sympathy. The technique is unusual, a technique he made distinctively his own. On cardboard (or some other porous material) he deliberately omitted the usual coating of size or plaster, intended to prevent oil from seeping through. His pigments were gouache, a kind of opaque watercolour, which he mixed with a volatile oil, and a dry, chalky colour, not unlike pastel.

Plates 89–90.
PIERRE BONNARD. 1867–1947. 'Nude Dressing' ('Nu à la toilette'). Oil. Brussels: Collection Georges Daelemans. © Sabam, Brussels; Spadem, Paris.

Bonnard and Vuillard were members of the Nabis, a doctrinaire group of French painters who were perhaps trying to formulate a claim implicit in a great deal of later 20th century painting — the claim that the paint — the oily, coloured material spread over a canvas and left to dry — is less important as a means to an end than it is in itself, as an assembly of colours and textures on a flat surface. By the middle of this century this doctrine, expressed more pretentiously and in a welter of words, was having a great success with critics and with the public cultivated by certain dealers. Bonnard, with Vuillard, in effect had abandoned it as long ago as 1905, when they evolved their own offshoot of Impressionism, for which the appropriate name of Intimism was found.

One characteristic of Intimism is that its subjects are so often domestic interiors, and another is that its colours are 'low keyed'; juxtaposed passages are never far apart in the spectrum order, and any intense contrast between bright colours is avoided. If this study of a girl completing her ablutions and about to dress herself is compared with 'Nude on a Sofa' (Plates 83–84) — although Renoir there restricts his colour range to an unusual degree — the distinction between Impressionism and Intimism should be clear. The Degas pastel, 'After the Bath (Plates 81–82), however, is almost as low keyed as the Bonnard; this reinforces the argument that Degas was not truly Impressionist in theory or in practice.

Plates 91–92.
HENRI MATISSE. 1869–1954. 'Loulou'. Oil. Private Collection. © Sabam, Brussels; Spadem, Paris.

Matisse lived for the last 40 years of his life on the French Riviera, a coast plentifully decorated with palm trees and with buildings decorated with brightly coloured stucco, so that it closely resembles North Africa, with which it has many historical connections. This affords a clue to an understanding of the artistic style of Matisse, who moved restlessly between the doctrines and practices of various schools and achieved no great success until in 1910 he saw an Exhibition of Near-Eastern art at Munich. Thereafter he adapted and worked out a style involving flat passages of bright colours with curving and often interlacing lines drawn in black or brown. Matisse compositions have often been compared to the abstract patterns known as 'arabesques'. The whole School of Paris, of which he was for several decades the leading practitioner next to Picasso, was predominantly decorative; it had little to do with history or religion or human relationships and aimed like a poster or a printed textile to please the eye without arousing the emotions.

Matisse had an experimental mind and a wonderful sense of design, of knowing where to place his lines and his colours within the picture area so that curiosity is first stimulated and ultimately satisfied. He belonged to the main tradition not only in his persistent devotion to drawing but in his parallel interest in the nude, even though, as here, he subordinated it to a decorative purpose. As a composition depending largely on a dominant diagonal set up by a naked body, 'Loulou' may be compared with the Annibale Carracci (Plates 51–52) and the Rubens (Plates 55–56).

Plates 93–94.
AMEDEO MODIGLIANI. 1884–1920. 'Nude'. Oil. London: Courtauld Institute of Art Galleries © Sabam, Brussels; Spadem, Paris.

Modigliani's short life is conventionally unconventional. Of Jewish descent and Italian birth, he revolted against his comfortably bourgeois upbringing and took himself off to Paris where he soon brought his life to a disastrous end through the customary dissipations of what was then romantically called bohemianism. Except when drink brought secret dissatisfactions to the surface, Modigliani seems to have been a gentle and pleasing character, and his work — sculptures as well as paintings and drawings — has never lost its seductive charm.

It has been said (as of Michelangelo) that his pictures have the quality of sculpture, but if so, the comparison should be with sculpture in low relief, which itself has the quality of drawing. It is from Botticelli and from the fresco painters of Tuscany that Modigliani, the Parisian, derives. He is a delineator and simplifier of nude forms, weaving the curved outlines into apparently spontaneous patterns within the rectangular area of the canvas. The face, downbent, in this splendid example is, perhaps unconsciously, reminiscent of dead faces in many a *quattrocento* pietà or martyrdom. One element in the Modigliani formula, an elongated neck set at an angle — it derives from Parmigianino and other Mannerists — is not to be found in this otherwise typical example.

Plates 95–96
PABLO PICASSO. b. 1881. 'Nude in the Forest'. Oil. Leningrad: Hermitage Museum. © Sabam, Brussels; Spadem, Paris.

In this sombre composition the figure is recognizably human and female and yet has some of the qualities of an abstract; it might almost be a primitive, even a pre-historic stone carving. Such an attempt to capture the moods of the remote past and of uncivilized people is, we recognize, characteristic of the art of our own time. This painting was done as long ago as 1908, which indicates one aspect of Picasso — as an innovator, a founder or early supporter of artistic 'movements'. In 1908 he had been seven years resident in Paris, was dissociating himself from the ideas of Matisse and the Fauves, and had struck up a friendship with Braque from which was soon to emerge the theory and practice of Cubism.

'Nude in the Forest' is influenced, perhaps, by Spanish sculptures but most of all by Cézanne, who had died two years earlier. By comparison with Picasso, Cézanne appears, to many people, to lack imagination, technical skill, and range and variety of subject. He is a painter made important by theorizing and, for good or for ill, he undoubtedly had a most powerful influence on other artists. Picasso is himself a great influencer, but by the time others are ready to follow his example he has begun new stylistic experiments. He has been likened to a chimera, a chameleon, and an insect — on the assumption that an insect lives wholly in the present moment, with no memory of the past and no anticipation of the future. However that may be, Picasso has immense gifts and is probably the most versatile painter in the whole history of art. Here he is seen, still in his twenties, putting Cézanne's precepts into more memorable practice than Cézanne ever could, and presenting the human face and the human body as shapes closely akin to 'the cube, the cylinder, and the cone'.

Plates 97–98.
MARCEL GROMAIRE. b. 1892. 'Les Lignes de la Main'. Oil. Paris: Museum of Modern Art. © Sabam, Brussels; Spadem, Paris.

Gromaire is an individualist. He goes his own way in art, absorbing 'influence' in small quantities as he feels he needs it but ignoring the innumerable movements and doctrines of the 20th century rather than either espousing or repudiating them. It is because of this, perhaps — because he does not easily fit into the verbose expositions of fashionable critics — that his name is less familiar than such names as Utrillo, Chagall, Soutine, Dufy.
Gromaire is classic. He constructs a picture so that it satisfies one's sense of logic, and he draws skilfully, decisively. Here the

idiom is 20th century with characteristics — geometric simplification of the faces and a blending of curves into angularities — that are peculiar to Gromaire. The theme, however, is timeless: two young women, probably prostitutes or 'show girls', are consulting an old fortune teller. The clock is a symbol of time and the alarms that time brings; the scissors indicate eventual death. The basic technique, dependent on strong delineations, has a long tradition behind it. As with the Modigliani (Plates 93–94) it goes back at least as far as Ancient Egypt.

Plates 99–100.
HENRY MOORE. b. 1898. 'King and Queen'. Bronze. London: Tate Gallery.

Henry Moore, recognized in most parts of the world as the leading British sculptor of today, uses both of the traditional methods of his craft: he carves, usually in stone, and he models shapes that are afterwards cast in metal. Otherwise he seems to break with tradition and to form his conceptions as if neither Renaissance nor Classical art had ever existed. His work, however, is rarely abstract; even in those carvings of recumbent figures, of which the centre is a scooped-out cavity, a minimum suggestion of natural forms is retained. Here the polished and incised surface of the bronze is in itself pleasing, and the distortions hardly impede our instant recognition of the figures as human and male and female. The skirt-like garments and the bare feet suggest either an ancient civilization or a primitive society of today, and the title of the piece is perhaps justified by the crown-like shapes on the heads.

What further significance may be drawn from the sculpture is more debatable. The 20th century has passed judgment on the art of the 19th and has rejected much that was undertaken with the loftiest intentions. In due course the 21st century will review works such as this, when they have lost the impact of novelty, and will no doubt reach a more objective assessment than any of us can hope for today.

Plates 101–102.
KAREL APPEL. b. 1921. Amsterdam. 'Machteld'. Oil. St. Louis, Missouri, U.S.A.: Mr. and Mrs. James W. Singer Collection.

In the middle decades of the 20th century the doctrine of 'painterliness' has been pushed to the point where oil paints that have been spread, with brush or knife, over a level surface have come to be regarded as artistically self-sufficient and self-explanatory. Nowadays a picture does not necessarily represent something (so that it is no longer necessary for an artist to be able to draw), and all it need express is something in the artist's mind of which he himself may be completely unaware. In the making of a picture the element that formerly would have been described as inspiration or imagination or improvisation has become all powerful, at the very moment that the representational purpose has been disavowed, along with the discipline of drawing. It is not surprising, therefore, that in the field of abstract design the carefully planned, 'geometric' composition has lately become less fashionable than swirls and sputters of paint achieved by chance or else by the artist's working in a state of frenzy or mental automatism.

A glance at Plates 101–102 will show that Karel Appel, one of the foremost experimental painters of the mid-century has some artistic kinship with certain abstract painters, and yet should not be classified with them; he retains at least one of the basic principles of traditional Western art. He organizes his pictures to represent, however crudely, something objective, something that exists outside his own mind. This 'Machteld', done in 1962, is one of a series and takes its name from the model. He has in fact addressed himself to the primary subjects of all humanist art over 3000 years — the naked human body and the human face. The difference, or one difference, lies in the vehement emphasis Mr. Appel gives to the ridged and multicoloured surface texture of the paint.